ABBREVIATED BLESSINGS BOOK
(SECOND EDITION)

A Collection of Short Prayers, Blessings, and Hymns
According to the Customs of the Karaite Jews,
Including Transliterations and English Translations

ספר ברכות מקוצר

קובץ תפילות, ברכות וזמירות מקוצרות,
כמנהג היהודים הקראים
כולל תעתיקים ותרגומים לאנגלית

THE KARAITE JEWS OF AMERICA

KaraiteJewsofAmerica@karaites.org
http://www.karaites.org

For additional books, please visit
www.TheKaraitePress.com

ISBN: 978-1-7330492-1-4

COVER DESIGN: Shimra Starr
TYPOGRAPHY: Raphaël Freeman MISTD, Renana Typesetting

Acknowledgments

The Karaite Jews of America is grateful to Neria Haroeh, who served as the editor and creative brain behind the First Edition of this Abbreviated Blessings Book. We take this opportunity to thank everyone who worked on this Second Edition, including Jeffrey Davis, Joel Davidi, James Walker, Nir Nissim, and Shawn Lichaa. We also thank everyone who contributed to or inspired the First Edition: Rav Hayim Levi, Rav Joseph Pessah, Rav Moshe Dabbach, Baruch Haroeh, Ovadia Gamil, Elie Moussa, David Ovadia, Shawn Lichaa, Fred Ovadia, Albert Farag, Noam Morad, Eli Shemuel, Rotem Cohen, Mark Levy, and many, many others.

Finally, we recognize that neither this Second Edition nor the First Edition would have been possible without the generous support of (i) Mrs. Hannah Levy and her children, who dedicated the First Edition in honor of her late husband, Isaac ben Joseph Chaim Levy, and (ii) the bequest of Zaki Joseph Lichaa, which funded this Second Edition.

Contents

Introduction

This book is virtually identical in substance to the First Edition. It is designed to assist you in learning and reciting blessings and prayers for everyday occasions. As in the First Edition, we have transliterated and translated the Hebrew text, with the hope of making it accessible to all. This Second Edition contains slight changes to the original translations, and we have updated the transliteration to better reflect how spoken Hebrew is taught in the United States.

The majority of these blessings come from Volume IV of the Vilna Karaite Siddur, published in 1891. Many of the blessings presented in both this edition and the First Edition were abbreviated in order to introduce the novice to reciting blessings. Among the items we did not shorten were the Kiddush for Friday evening, the Kiddush for Saturday morning, the blessings for Havdalah, the blessings for the sick, the blessings in memory of the departed, and the blessing before meals.

As in the First Edition, we have included blessings composed by Neria Haroeh. For example, he composed the prayer one recites during difficult times, which he based on a prayer written by the late Hakham Tuvia Levy-Babovich. Neria also composed the prayer before taking a test. He also composed the prayer for having worthy friends, which he based on the prayer for difficult times. He composed the blessings by parents for their children, which he based upon the Biblical blessings of Jacob to Menashe and Ephraim (see Genesis 48) and Isaac to Jacob (see Genesis 28). We have slightly updated the blessing for daughters to include references to Ruth, Leah, and Rachel.

In the First Edition, the song Matoḳ Devar Torah was attributed to the Karaite Sage Moses Baghi. This is almost certainly a misattribution, for this song appears in Rabbanite sources as well, making it highly unlikely that it is of Karaite origin. In this edition, we have simply attributed it to Rabbi Moshe (based on the acrostic), as scholars are uncertain of the actual author's identity.

Finally, we have added an asterisk (*) before the parts of the blessings and prayers meant to be recited by the congregation (as opposed to the person performing the blessing).

ABOUT THE FORMAT The reader will note that we have set the Hebrew and English transliteration on the same line, opposing each other, with the Hebrew on the left and the English on the right. While this layout may be new to many of our readers, we chose it because it offers several advantages. Most importantly, the beginning of every line (Hebrew and transliteration) are clearly visible to the reader because they are in the center of each page. We also typeset the beginning of prayers and key passages in red. This allows the reader to easily identify upcoming passages. Finally, we broke up longer passages (even parts of the same blessing) into smaller units to allow us to typeset the translation close in space to the Hebrew text.

In typesetting this book, we have opted for aesthetics and practicality over historical consistency. For example, many passages that are broken up into separate paragraphs or are identified with red text are parts of larger prayers that historically would have been printed continuously as part of a single paragraph or section. We take very seriously our role in preserving Karaite liturgy; so, we endeavored to preserve the substance of our liturgy while presenting a new layout that is more digestible to English readers.

ABOUT THE TRANSLITERATION We have transliterated the Hebrew text according to an Egyptian/Israeli Karaite pronunciation system. While this transliteration reflects how Karaites actually pronounce these blessings, prayers, and songs, we note that, on occasion, this pronunciation breaks the meter of the poems. For example, in *Matoḳ Devar Tora*, the community reads the third line of the third stanza as "ha'omerim tamid", whereas the meter dictates that it be read as "ha'omrim tamid".

* * *

Please note: This book contains God's personal name and should be treated with great care. If you do not plan to use it anymore, we respectfully ask that you place it in a genizah, donate it, or return it to the Karaite Jews of America.

About the Transliteration

We have endeavored to create a simple transliteration scheme. To further assist the reader, we provide the following:

Consonants

א	Aleph	Indicated by the corresponding vowel
בּ	Beth (hard)	b
ב	Beth (soft)	v
גּ	Gimmel (hard)	g
ג	Gimmel (soft)	ḡ
ד	Daleth (whether hard or soft)	d
ה	Hé	h (Note: Never indicated when silent.)
ו	Vav	v
ז	Zayin	z
ח	Ḥeth	ḥ
ט	Ṭeth	t
י	Yod	y, i (Note: Never indicated when silent.)
כּ	Kaf (hard)	k
כ	Kaf (soft)	ch
ל	Lamed	l

מ	Mem	m
נ	Nun	n
ס	Samekh	s
ע	‘Ayin	‘
פּ	Pé	p
פ	Fé	f
צ	Tsadi	ts
ק	Quf	ḳ
ר	Resh	r
שׁ	Shin	sh
שׂ	Sin	s
ת	Tav (whether hard or soft)	t

Vowels

ַ ָ ֲ	Pataḥ, Qamets gadol, Ḥaṭaf-pathaḥ	a
ֵ ֶ ְ ֱ	TSeré, Segol, Sheva, Ḥataf-segol	e
ִ	Ḥireq	i

וֹ ָ	Ḥolem, Qamets qaṭan	o
וּ ֻ	Shuruq, Qubbuts	u

Additional Notes

1. Final tseré and segol are indicated as "é" so that the English reader will not misread the final "e" as silent. Thus, to prevent the English reader from reading מִינֵי as the English word "mine," we have rendered it as miné. This rendering is not intended to indicate that the syllable should be stressed.
2. Doubled consonants (i.e., those with dagesh ḥazaq) are indicated with the doubling of the letter in English. Thus, חֻקִּים = ḥukkim. When the consonant is indicated in English with two characters – sh or ts – we have put a hyphen between the repetitions of this cluster; thus, חִצִּים = ḥits-tsim; אִשָּׁה = ish-sha.
3. When the consonant ṭeth or tav, both of which are represented by the letter *t*, is followed immediately by hé, we have placed a hyphen between them so that the English reader will not read them as "th," as in the English word "thin." Thus: וּתְהִלָּה = "ut-hilla." We have also placed a hyphen to separate other English consonants, where necessary to avoid mispronunciation. We have not done so when a ḥeth follows the teth or tav.
4. When our transliteration yields two consecutive English vowels that may mistakenly be read as one sound, we have placed an apostrophe between them. Thus: וְאֶת = ve'et.
5. When a final yod is preceded by a qamets or pataḥ, we have transliterated it as an "i". For example, אֱלֹהַי is transliterated as "Elohai" and not "Elohay", so as to avoid misreading the word as "Elohé" (אֱלֹהֵי).

Weekday Blessings over Food & Beverage

FOR WINE (ON WEEKDAYS)

הוֹדוּ לַיהוָה כִּי־טוֹב,	Hodu ladonai ki tov,
★ כִּי לְעוֹלָם חַסְדּוֹ:	★ Ki le'olam ḥasdo:
הוֹדוּ לֵאלֹהֵי הָאֱלֹהִים,	Hodu lelohé ha'elohim,
★ כִּי לְעוֹלָם חַסְדּוֹ:	★ Ki le'olam ḥasdo:
הוֹדוּ לַאֲדֹנֵי הָאֲדֹנִים	Hodu la'adoné ha'adonim
★ כִּי לְעוֹלָם חַסְדּוֹ:	★ Ki le'olam ḥasdo:
בָּרוּךְ אַתָּה יְהוָה אֱלֹהֵינוּ מֶלֶךְ	Baruch atta Adonai Elohenu melech
הָעוֹלָם הַנּוֹתֵן לָנוּ שָׂשׂוֹן וְשִׂמְחָה	ha'olam hannoten lanu sason vesimḥa
וּבוֹרֵא פְּרִי הַגָּפֶן:	uvoré peri haggafen:
★ אָמֵן:	★ Amen:

GIVE THANKS to Adonai, for He is good,
★ For His loving-kindness is everlasting.

GIVE THANKS to the God of gods,
★ For His loving-kindness is everlasting.

GIVE THANKS to the Lord of lords,
For His loving-kindness is everlasting.

BLESSED are You, Adonai, our God, King
of the universe, Who gives us joy and happiness
and creates the fruit of the vine.
★ Amen.

FOR BREAD

בָּרוּךְ אַתָּה יְהוָה אֱלֹהֵינוּ מֶלֶךְ
הָעוֹלָם הַמּוֹצִיא לֶחֶם מִן הָאָרֶץ׃

Baruch atta Adonai Elohenu melech
haʿolam hammotsi leḥem min haʾarets:

BLESSED *are You, Adonai, our God, King of the universe, Who brings bread out of the earth.*

FOR PASTRIES (INCLUDING CAKES)

בָּרוּךְ אַתָּה יְהוָה אֱלֹהֵינוּ מֶלֶךְ
הָעוֹלָם בּוֹרֵא מִינֵי מְזוֹנוֹת׃

Baruch atta Adonai Elohenu melech
haʿolam boré miné mezonot:

BLESSED *are You, Adonai, our God, King of the universe, Who creates food of all kinds.*

FOR FRUITS OF THE TREE

בָּרוּךְ אַתָּה יְהוָה אֱלֹהֵינוּ מֶלֶךְ
הָעוֹלָם בּוֹרֵא פְּרִי הָעֵץ׃

Baruch atta Adonai Elohenu melech
haʿolam boré peri haʿets:

BLESSED *are You, Adonai, our God, King of the universe, Who creates the fruit of the tree.*

FOR FRUITS AND VEGETABLES OF THE EARTH

בָּרוּךְ אַתָּה יְהוָה אֱלֹהֵינוּ מֶלֶךְ
הָעוֹלָם בּוֹרֵא פְּרִי הָאֲדָמָה׃

Baruch atta Adonai Elohenu melech
haʿolam boré peri haʾadama:

BLESSED *are You, Adonai, our God, King of the universe, Who creates the fruit of the earth.*

FOR OTHER FOODS

For any drink (except wine) and for certain foods, such as meat, fish, eggs, cheese, and candy.

בָּרוּךְ אַתָּה יְהוָה אֱלֹהֵינוּ מֶלֶךְ
הָעוֹלָם שֶׁהַכֹּל נִהְיָה בִּדְבָרוֹ׃

Baruch atta Adonai Elohenu melech
haʿolam shehakkol nihya bidvaro:

BLESSED *are You, Adonai, our God, King of the universe, by Whose word everything exists.*

BIRKAT HAMAZON – WEEKDAY (BLESSING AFTER A MEAL)

יוֹדוּךָ יְהוָה כָּל־מַעֲשֶׂיךָ,	Yoducha Adonai kol maʿasecha,
וַחֲסִידֶיךָ יְבָרְכוּכָה: נוֹדֶה לַיהוָה	vaḥasidecha yevarechucha: Nodé ladonai
חַסְדּוֹ, וְנִפְלְאוֹתָיו לִבְנֵי אָדָם: כִּי־	ḥasdo, venifle'otav livné adam: Ki
הִשְׂבִּיעַ נֶפֶשׁ שֹׁקֵקָה, וְנֶפֶשׁ רְעֵבָה	hisbiaʿ nefesh shoḳeḳa, venefesh reʿeva
מִלֵּא־טוֹב: לֹא־יֵבֹשׁוּ בְּעֵת רָעָה,	millé tov: Lo yevoshu beʿet raʿa,
וּבִימֵי רְעָבוֹן יִשְׂבָּעוּ:	uvimé reʿavon yisbaʿu:
וְאָכַלְתָּ וְשָׂבָעְתָּ, וּבֵרַכְתָּ אֶת־יְהוָה	Ve'achalta vesavaʿta uverachta et Adonai
אֱלֹהֶיךָ, עַל־הָאָרֶץ הַטֹּבָה אֲשֶׁר	Elohecha, ʿal ha'arets hattova asher
נָתַן־לָךְ:	natan lach:

ALL YOUR WORKS shall give thanks to You, Adonai, and Your godly ones shall bless You. We praise Adonai for His loving-kindness, and for His wondrous deeds for mankind: for He satisfies the longing soul, and fills the hungry soul with goodness. They will not be shamed in times of calamity; and in days of famine, they will be satisfied.

YOU WILL EAT and you will be satisfied, and you shall bless Adonai, your God, for the good land, which He has given you.

בֵּית יִשְׂרָאֵל בָּרְכוּ אֶת־יְהוָה,	Bet Yisra'el barechu et Adonai,
★ בָּרוּךְ יהוה:	★ Baruch Adonai:
בֵּית אַהֲרֹן בָּרְכוּ אֶת־יְהוָה:	Bet Aharon barechu et Adonai,
★ בָּרוּךְ יהוה:	★ Baruch Adonai:

O HOUSE OF ISRAEL, bless Adonai!
Blessed be Adonai!

O HOUSE OF AARON, bless Adonai!
Blessed be Adonai!

בֵּית הַלֵּוִי בָּרְכוּ אֶת־יְהוָה,	Bet Hallevi barechu et Adonai,
★ בָּרוּךְ יהוה:	★ Baruch Adonai:
יִרְאֵי יְהוָה בָּרְכוּ אֶת־יְהוָה:	Yiré Adonai barechu et Adonai,
★ בָּרוּךְ יהוה:	★ Baruch Adonai:
בָּרוּךְ יְהוָה ׀ מִצִּיּוֹן שֹׁכֵן	Baruch Adonai mits-tsiyyon shochen
יְרוּשָׁלָ͏ִם	Yerushalayim,
★ הַלְלוּיָהּ:	★ Haleluyah:
יְהוָה עֹז לְעַמּוֹ יִתֵּן,	Adonai ʿoz leʿammo yitten,
★ יְהוָה ׀ יְבָרֵךְ אֶת־עַמּוֹ בַשָּׁלוֹם:	★ Adonai yevarech et ʿammo vash-shalom:
בָּרוּךְ יְהוָה לְעוֹלָם,	Baruch Adonai leʿolam,
★ אָמֵן ׀ וְאָמֵן:	★ Amen veʾamen:

O HOUSE OF LEVI, bless Adonai!
★Blessed be Adonai!

O THOSE WHO FEAR Adonai, bless Adonai!
★Blessed be Adonai!

BLESSED be Adonai from Zion, He who dwells in Jerusalem!
★Halleluyah.

ADONAI will give strength to His people;
★Adonai will bless His people with peace.

BLESSED be Adonai forevermore;
★Amen, and Amen.

Blessings for Shabbat

ברכות ליום השבת

EREV SHABBAT KIDDUSH OVER WINE AND BLESSING OVER CHALLAH

Raise the Kiddush cup and say:

עֵת לְהַקְדִּישׁ, וַיְכֻלּוּ הַשָּׁמַיִם	ʿEt lehaḳdish, Vaychullu hash-shamayim
וְהָאָרֶץ וְכָל־צְבָאָם: וַיְכַל אֱלֹהִים	veha'arets vechol tseva'am: Vaychal Elohim
בַּיּוֹם הַשְּׁבִיעִי מְלַאכְתּוֹ אֲשֶׁר	bayyom hash-sheviʿi melachto asher
עָשָׂה, וַיִּשְׁבֹּת בַּיּוֹם הַשְּׁבִיעִי,	ʿasa, vayyishbot bayyom hash-sheviʿi,
מִכָּל־מְלַאכְתּוֹ אֲשֶׁר עָשָׂה: וַיְבָרֶךְ	mikkol melachto asher ʿasa: Vayvarech
אֱלֹהִים אֶת־יוֹם הַשְּׁבִיעִי וַיְקַדֵּשׁ	Elohim et yom hash-sheviʿi vayḳaddesh
אֹתוֹ כִּי בוֹ שָׁבַת מִכָּל־מְלַאכְתּוֹ	oto ki vo shavat mikkol melachto
אֲשֶׁר־בָּרָא אֱלֹהִים לַעֲשׂוֹת:	asher bara Elohim laʿasot:

A TIME TO SANCTIFY: *Heaven and earth, and all their components, were thus completed. God finished on the seventh day all the work that He had done. He thus ceased on the seventh day from all His work that He had been doing. Then God blessed the seventh day, and He declared it to be holy, for it was on this day that God ceased from all His work that He had been creating.*

וּבָרוּךְ אֱלֹהֵינוּ מֶלֶךְ הָעוֹלָם אֲשֶׁר	Uvaruch Elohenu melech haʿolam asher
בָּרָא עֵץ הַגֶּפֶן וּמִיֵּינוֹ מְשַׂמֵּחַ	bara ʿets haggefen umiyyeno mesamme'aḥ
לְבַב בְּנֵי הָאָדָם: כַּכָּתוּב, וְיַיִן ׀	levav bené ha'adam: Kakkatuv, veyayin
יְשַׂמַּח לְבַב־אֱנוֹשׁ לְהַצְהִיל פָּנִים	yesammaḥ levav enosh lehats-hil panim
מִשָּׁמֶן, וְלֶחֶם לְבַב־אֱנוֹשׁ יִסְעָד:	mish-shamen, veleḥem levav enosh yisʿad:

AND BLESSED *be our God, King of the universe, Who creates the grapevine, and from its wine gladdens the heart of the children of man. As it is written: And wine makes man's heart happy, and his face shinier than oil, and bread strengthens man's heart.*

בָּרוּךְ אַתָּה יְהוָֹה אֱלֹהֵינוּ מֶלֶךְ
הָעוֹלָם הַמְבָרֵךְ וְהַמְקַדֵּשׁ אֶת
יוֹם הַשַּׁבָּת לְעַמּוֹ יִשְׂרָאֵל:
★ אָמֵן:

Baruch atta Adonai Elohenu melech
ha'olam hamevarech vehameḳaddesh et
yom hash-shabbat le'ammo Yisra'el:
★ Amen:

וּבָרוּךְ אֱלֹהֵינוּ מֶלֶךְ הָעוֹלָם
הַנּוֹתֵן לָנוּ שָׂשׂוֹן וְשִׂמְחָה וּבוֹרֵא
פְּרִי הַגָּפֶן:
★ אָמֵן:

Uvaruch Elohenu melech ha'olam
hannoten lanu sason vesimḥa uvoré
peri haggafen:
★ Amen:

BLESSED are You, Adonai, our God, King of the universe, Who blesses the Shabbat Day and declares it holy for His people, Israel. ★Amen.

AND BLESSED be our God, King of the universe, Who gives us joy and happiness, and creates the fruit of the vine. ★ Amen.

Blessing over The Bread (Challah):

בָּרוּךְ אַתָּה יְהוָֹה אֱלֹהֵינוּ מֶלֶךְ
הָעוֹלָם הַמּוֹצִיא לֶחֶם מִן הָאָרֶץ:
★ אָמֵן:

Baruch atta Adonai Elohenu melech
ha'olam hammotsi leḥem min ha'arets:
★ Amen:

EREV SHABBAT BIRKAT HAMAZON (BLESSING AFTER A MEAL)

וְשָׁמְרוּ בְנֵי־יִשְׂרָאֵל אֶת־הַשַּׁבָּת	Veshameru vené Yisra'el et hash-shabbat
לַעֲשׂוֹת אֶת־הַשַּׁבָּת לְדֹרֹתָם בְּרִית	la'asot et hash-shabbat ledorotam berit
עוֹלָם: בֵּינִי וּבֵין בְּנֵי יִשְׂרָאֵל אוֹת	'olam: Beni uven bené Yisra'el ot
הִוא לְעֹלָם, כִּי־שֵׁשֶׁת יָמִים עָשָׂה	hi le'olam, ki sheshet yamim 'asa
יְהֹוָה אֶת־הַשָּׁמַיִם וְאֶת־הָאָרֶץ,	Adonai et hash-shamayim ve'et ha'arets,
וּבַיּוֹם הַשְּׁבִיעִי שָׁבַת וַיִּנָּפַשׁ:	uvayyom hash-shevi'i shavat vayyinnafash:

AND THE CHILDREN OF ISRAEL SHALL KEEP the Shabbat day, making it a day of rest for all generations, as an eternal covenant. It is a sign between Me and the children of Israel that for six days Adonai made heaven and earth, but on the seventh day He ceased from work and rested.

וַיַּקְהֵל מֹשֶׁה אֶת־כָּל־עֲדַת בְּנֵי	Vayyakhel Moshé et kol 'adat bené
יִשְׂרָאֵל וַיֹּאמֶר אֲלֵהֶם, אֵלֶּה	Yisra'el vayyomer alehem, ellé
הַדְּבָרִים אֲשֶׁר־צִוָּה יְהֹוָה לַעֲשֹׂת	haddevarim asher tsivva Adonai la'asot
אֹתָם: שֵׁשֶׁת יָמִים תֵּעָשֶׂה מְלָאכָה,	otam: Sheshet yamim te'asé melacha,
וּבַיּוֹם הַשְּׁבִיעִי יִהְיֶה לָכֶם	uvayyom hash-shevi'i yihyé lachem
קֹדֶשׁ שַׁבַּת שַׁבָּתוֹן לַיהֹוָה,	kodesh shabbat shabbaton ladonai,
כָּל־הָעֹשֶׂה בוֹ מְלָאכָה יוּמָת:	kol ha'osé vo melacha yumat:
לֹא־תְבַעֲרוּ אֵשׁ בְּכֹל מֹשְׁבֹתֵיכֶם,	Lo teva'aru esh bechol moshevotechem,
בְּיוֹם הַשַּׁבָּת:	beyom hash-shabbat:

AND MOSES ASSEMBLED the entire congregation of the children of Israel, and said to them, "These are the words that Adonai has commanded – to do them. Six days shall work be done, but on the seventh day there shall be to you a holy day, a sabbath of rest to Adonai. Whosoever does work therein shall be put to death. Do not burn any fires throughout your habitations on the Shabbat day."

אֶת־שַׁבְּתֹתַי תִּשְׁמֹרוּ וּמִקְדָּשִׁי
תִּירָאוּ, אֲנִי יְהוָה: אִישׁ אִמּוֹ וְאָבִיו
תִּירָאוּ, וְאֶת־שַׁבְּתֹתַי תִּשְׁמֹרוּ, אֲנִי
יְהוָה אֱלֹהֵיכֶם:

Et shabbetotai tishmoru, umiḳdashi
tira'u, ani Adonai: Ish immo ve'aviv
tira'u, ve'et shabbetotai tishmoru, ani
Adonai elohechem:

KEEP MY SABBATHS and revere My sanctuary; I am Adonai. Each person shall revere their mother and father, and shall keep my Sabbaths. I am Adonai, your God.

וַעֲבַדְתֶּם אֵת יְהוָה אֱלֹהֵיכֶם, וּבֵרַךְ
אֶת־לַחְמְךָ וְאֶת־מֵימֶיךָ, וַהֲסִרֹתִי
מַחֲלָה מִקִּרְבֶּךָ: וּבָתִּים מְלֵאִים
כָּל־טוּב אֲשֶׁר לֹא־מִלֵּאתָ וּבֹרֹת
חֲצוּבִים אֲשֶׁר לֹא־חָצַבְתָּ כְּרָמִים
וְזֵיתִים אֲשֶׁר לֹא־נָטָעְתָּ וְאָכַלְתָּ
וְשָׂבָעְתָּ:

Va'avadtem et Adonai Elohechem, uverach
et laḥmecha ve'et memecha, vehasiroti
maḥala miḳḳirbecha: Uvattim mele'im
kol tuv asher lo milleta uvorot
ḥatsuvim asher lo ḥatsavta keramim
vezetim asher lo nata'ta, ve'achalta
vesava'ta:

YOU WILL THEN SERVE Adonai, your God, and He will bless your bread and your water, and I will banish sickness from among you. And houses full of all good things, which you did not fill, and cisterns hewn out, which you did not hew, vineyards and olive-trees, which you did not plant, and you shall eat and be satisfied.

וְאָכַלְתָּ וְשָׂבָעְתָּ, וּבֵרַכְתָּ אֶת־יְהוָה
אֱלֹהֶיךָ עַל־הָאָרֶץ הַטֹּבָה אֲשֶׁר
נָתַן־לָךְ:

Ve'achalta, vesava'ta, uverachta et Adonai
Elohecha 'al ha'arets hattova asher
natan lach:

WHEN YOU HAVE EATEN and are satisfied, then you shall bless Adonai, your God, for the good land that He has given you.

בֵּית יִשְׂרָאֵל בָּרְכוּ אֶת־יְהוָה,
★ בָּרוּךְ יהוה:

Bet Yisra'el barechu et Adonai,
★ Baruch Adonai:

BLESS ADONAI, O HOUSE OF ISRAEL!
★ Blessed be Adonai!

בֵּית אַהֲרֹן בָּרְכוּ אֶת־יְהוָה׃	Bet Aharon barechu et Adonai,
★ בָּרוּךְ יהוה׃	★ Baruch Adonai:
בֵּית הַלֵּוִי בָּרְכוּ אֶת־יְהוָה,	Bet Hallevi barechu et Adonai,
★ בָּרוּךְ יהוה׃	★ Baruch Adonai:
יִרְאֵי יְהוָה בָּרְכוּ אֶת־יְהוָה׃	Yiré Adonai barechu et Adonai,
★ בָּרוּךְ יהוה׃	Baruch Adonai:
בָּרוּךְ יְהוָה ׀ מִצִּיּוֹן שֹׁכֵן	Baruch Adonai mits-Tsiyyon shochen
יְרוּשָׁלָםִ,	Yerushalayim,
★ הַלְלוּיָהּ׃	Haleluyah:
יְהוָה עֹז לְעַמּוֹ יִתֵּן	Adonai ʿoz leʿammo yitten,
★ יְהוָה ׀ יְבָרֵךְ אֶת־עַמּוֹ בַשָּׁלוֹם׃	Adonai yevarech et ʿammo vash-shalom:
בָּרוּךְ יְהוָה לְעוֹלָם,	Baruch Adonai leʿolam,
★ אָמֵן ׀ וְאָמֵן׃	Amen veʾamen:

BLESS ADONAI, O HOUSE OF AARON!

★ *Blessed be Adonai!*

BLESS ADONAI, O HOUSE OF LEVI!

★ *Blessed be Adonai!*

O YOU WHO FEAR Adonai, bless Adonai.

★ *Blessed be Adonai!*

BLESSED BE Adonai from Zion, He who dwells at Jerusalem!

★ *Halleluyah.*

ADONAI will give strength to His people;

★ *Adonai will bless His people with peace.*

BLESSED be Adonai forevermore;

★ *Amen, and Amen.*

SHABBAT DAY KIDDUSH OVER WINE AND BLESSING OVER CHALLAH

Raise the Kiddush cup and say:

הוֹדוּ לַיהוָה כִּי־טוֹב, — Hodu ladonai ki tov,

★ כִּי לְעוֹלָם חַסְדּוֹ: — ★ Ki le'olam ḥasdo:

הוֹדוּ לֵאלֹהֵי הָאֱלֹהִים, — Hodu lelohé ha'elohim,

★ כִּי לְעוֹלָם חַסְדּוֹ: — ★ Ki le'olam ḥasdo:

הוֹדוּ לַאֲדֹנֵי הָאֲדֹנִים — Hodu la'adoné ha'adonim

★ כִּי לְעוֹלָם חַסְדּוֹ: — ★ Ki le'olam ḥasdo:

GIVE THANKS to Adonai, for He is good,
★ For His loving-kindness is everlasting.

GIVE THANKS to the God of gods,
★ For His loving-kindness is everlasting.

GIVE THANKS to the Lord of lords,
★ For His loving-kindness is everlasting.

וּבָרוּךְ אֱלֹהֵינוּ מֶלֶךְ הָעוֹלָם, אֲשֶׁר
בֵּרַךְ וְקִדֵּשׁ אֶת יוֹם הַשְּׁבִיעִי
מִכָּל הַיָּמִים: כַּכָּתוּב, וַיְבָרֶךְ
אֱלֹהִים אֶת־יוֹם הַשְּׁבִיעִי וַיְקַדֵּשׁ
אֹתוֹ, כִּי בוֹ שָׁבַת מִכָּל־מְלַאכְתּוֹ,
אֲשֶׁר־בָּרָא אֱלֹהִים לַעֲשׂוֹת:

Uvaruch Elohenu melech ha'olam, asher
berach veḳiddesh et yom hash-shevi'i
mikkol hayyamim: Kakkatuv, vayvarech
Elohim et yom hash-shevi'i vayḳaddesh
oto, ki vo shavat mikkol melachto,
asher bara Elohim la'asot:

AND BLESSED be our God, King of the universe, Who blessed and made holy the seventh day from all the days. As it is written: God blessed the seventh day, and He declared it to be holy, for it was on this day that God ceased from all the work that He had been creating.

וּבָרוּךְ אֱלֹהֵינוּ מֶלֶךְ הָעוֹלָם אֲשֶׁר
בָּרָא עֵץ הַגֶּפֶן וּמִיֵּינוֹ מְשַׂמֵּחַ
לְבַב בְּנֵי הָאָדָם: כַּכָּתוּב, וְיַיִן ׀
יְשַׂמַּח לְבַב־אֱנוֹשׁ לְהַצְהִיל פָּנִים
מִשָּׁמֶן, וְלֶחֶם לְבַב־אֱנוֹשׁ יִסְעָד:

Uvaruch Elohenu melech ha'olam asher
bara 'ets haggefen umiyyeno mesamme'aḥ
levav bené ha'adam: Kakkatuv, veyayin
yesammaḥ levav enosh lehats-hil panim
mish-shamen, veleḥem levav enosh yis'ad:

בָּרוּךְ אַתָּה יְהוָֹה אֱלֹהֵינוּ מֶלֶךְ
הָעוֹלָם הַמְבָרֵךְ וְהַמְקַדֵּשׁ אֶת
יוֹם הַשַּׁבָּת לְעַמּוֹ יִשְׂרָאֵל:
⋆ אָמֵן:

Baruch atta Adonai Elohenu melech
ha'olam hamevarech vehameḳaddesh et
yom hash-shabbat le'ammo Yisra'el:
⋆ Amen:

וּבָרוּךְ אֱלֹהֵינוּ מֶלֶךְ הָעוֹלָם
הַנּוֹתֵן לָנוּ שָׂשׂוֹן וְשִׂמְחָה וּבוֹרֵא
פְּרִי הַגָּפֶן:
⋆ אָמֵן:

Uvaruch Elohenu melech ha'olam
hannoten lanu sason vesimḥa uvoré
peri haggafen:
⋆ Amen:

AND BLESSED be our God, King of the universe, Who creates the grapevine, and from its wine gladdens the heart of children of man, as it is written: And wine makes man's heart happy, and his face shinier than oil, and bread strengthens man's heart.

BLESSED are You, Adonai, our God, King of the universe, Who blesses the Shabbat Day and declares it holy for His people, Israel.

⋆ *Amen.*

AND BLESSED be our God, King of the universe, Who gives us joy and happiness and Who creates the fruit of the vine.

⋆ *Amen.*

Blessing over Challah:

בָּרוּךְ אַתָּה יְהוָֹה אֱלֹהֵינוּ מֶלֶךְ
הָעוֹלָם הַמּוֹצִיא לֶחֶם מִן הָאָרֶץ:
⋆ אָמֵן:

Baruch atta Adonai Elohenu melech
ha'olam hamotsi leḥem min ha'arets:
⋆ Amen:

BLESSED are You, Adonai, our God, King of the universe, Who brings bread out of the earth.

⋆ *Amen.*

SHABBAT DAY BIRKAT HAMAZON (BLESSING AFTER A MEAL)

טוֹב־יְהוָה לַכֹּל, וְרַחֲמָיו	Tov Adonai lakkol, veraḥamav
עַל־כָּל־מַעֲשָׂיו׃	ʿal kol maʿasav:
שֶׁבְּשִׁפְלֵנוּ זָכַר לָנוּ,	Shebbeshiflenu zachar lanu,
★ כִּי לְעוֹלָם חַסְדּוֹ׃	Ki leʿolam ḥasdo:
וַיִּפְרְקֵנוּ מִצָּרֵינוּ,	Vayyifreḳenu mits-tsarenu,
★ כִּי לְעוֹלָם חַסְדּוֹ׃	Ki leʿolam ḥasdo:
בָּרוּךְ הַנֹּתֵן לֶחֶם לְכָל־בָּשָׂר,	Baruch hannoten leḥem lechol basar,
★ כִּי לְעוֹלָם חַסְדּוֹ׃	Ki leʿolam ḥasdo:
הוֹדוּ לְאֵל הַשָּׁמָיִם,	Hodu le'El hash-shamayim,
★ כִּי לְעוֹלָם חַסְדּוֹ׃	Ki leʿolam ḥasdo:
יְהִי־חַסְדְּךָ יְהוָה עָלֵינוּ,	Yehi ḥasdecha Adonai ʿalenu,
★ כַּאֲשֶׁר יִחַלְנוּ לָךְ׃	Ka'asher yiḥalnu lach:
בָּרוּךְ יְהוָה לְעוֹלָם,	Baruch Adonai leʿolam
★ אָמֵן ׀ וְאָמֵן׃	Amen ve'amen:

ADONAI IS GOOD to all; and His mercy is over all His works.
Who remembered us in our lowly state;
★ *For His loving-kindness endures forever.*

AND HAS RESCUED US from our adversaries;
★ *For His loving-kindness endures forever.*

BLESSED be He who gives bread to all flesh;
★ *For His loving-kindness endures forever.*

GIVE THANKS to God of the heavens;
★ *For His loving-kindness endures forever.*

LET YOUR LOVING-KINDNESS, O Adonai, be upon us,
According as we have hoped in You.

BLESSED be Adonai forevermore;
★ *Amen, and Amen.*

For an abbreviated blessing, omit until the middle of the next page

בָּרוּךְ אַתָּה יְהוָה אֱלֹהֵי יִשְׂרָאֵל	Baruch atta Adonai Elohé Yisra'el
אָבִינוּ, מֵעוֹלָם וְעַד־עוֹלָם: לְךָ	avinu, meʿolam veʿad ʿolam: Lecha
יְהוָה הַגְּדֻלָּה וְהַגְּבוּרָה	Adonai haggedulla vehaggevura
וְהַתִּפְאֶרֶת וְהַנֵּצַח וְהַהוֹד כִּי־כֹל	vehattiferet vehannetsaḥ vehahod ki chol
בַּשָּׁמַיִם וּבָאָרֶץ, לְךָ יְהוָה	bash-shamayim uva'arets, lecha Adonai
הַמַּמְלָכָה וְהַמִּתְנַשֵּׂא	hammamlecha vehammitnassé
לְכֹל ׀ לְרֹאשׁ: וְהָעֹשֶׁר וְהַכָּבוֹד	lechol lerosh: Vehaʿosher vehakkavod
מִלְּפָנֶיךָ וְאַתָּה מוֹשֵׁל בַּכֹּל	millefanecha ve'atta moshel bakkol
וּבְיָדְךָ כֹּחַ וּגְבוּרָה, וּבְיָדְךָ	uvyadecha ko'aḥ uḡvura uvyadecha
לְגַדֵּל וּלְחַזֵּק לַכֹּל: וְעַתָּה אֱלֹהֵינוּ	leḡaddel ulḥazzeḳ lakkol: Veʿatta Elohenu
מוֹדִים אֲנַחְנוּ לָךְ, וּמְהַלְלִים	modim anaḥnu lach, umhalelim
לְשֵׁם תִּפְאַרְתֶּךָ: וַאֲנַחְנוּ ׀ נְבָרֵךְ יָהּ	leshem tifartecha: Va'anaḥnu nevarech Yah
מֵעַתָּה וְעַד־עוֹלָם, הַלְלוּ־יָהּ: עֵינֵי־	meʿatta veʿad ʿolam, halelu-Yah: ʿEné
כֹל אֵלֶיךָ יְשַׂבֵּרוּ, וְאַתָּה נוֹתֵן־	chol elecha yesabberu, ve-atta noten
לָהֶם אֶת־אָכְלָם בְּעִתּוֹ: פּוֹתֵחַ אֶת־	lahem et ochlam beʿitto: Pote'aḥ et
יָדֶךָ, וּמַשְׂבִּיעַ לְכָל־חַי רָצוֹן:	yadecha, umasbiaʿ lechol ḥai ratson:

BLESSED BE YOU, *O Adonai, the God of our father Israel, for ever and ever. Yours, O Adonai, is the greatness and the power, and the glory, and the victory, and the majesty; for all that is in the heavens and in the earth is Yours; Yours is the kingdom, O Adonai, and You are exalted as head above all. Both riches and honor come of You, and You rule over all; and in Your hand is power and might; and in Your hand it is to make great, and to give strength unto all. Now therefore, our God, we thank You, and praise Your glorious name. Indeed, we will bless Yah, now and forever. The eyes of all wait for You, and You give them their food in due time. You open Your hand and satisfy every living thing with favor.*

רָצוֹן תְּשַׂבְּעֵנוּ, וְרָזוֹן הַעֲבֵר	Ratson tesabbeʿenu verazon haʿaver
מִמֶּנּוּ, וְהַטְרִיפֵנוּ לֶחֶם חֻקֵּנוּ,	mimmennu, vehatrifenu leḥem ḥuḳḳenu,
וְשֻׁלְחָנְךָ עָרוּךְ לַכֹּל: בְּאֶרֶךְ	veshulḥanecha ʿaroch lakkol: Beʾerech
אַפְּךָ וּבִגְמִילוּת חֲסָדֶיךָ אָנוּ חַיִּים	appecha uviḡmilut ḥasadecha anu ḥayyim
וְקַיָּמִים, וּמִפְּתִיחַת יָדֶךָ: כִּי	veḳayyamim, umippetiḥat yadecha: Ki
אַתָּה הוּא זָן וּמְפַרְנֵס וּמְכַלְכֵּל לַכֹּל,	atta hu zan umfarnes umchalkel lakkol,
וּמֵכִין מָזוֹן וּמִחְיָה לְכָל בְּרִיּוֹתֶיךָ	umechin mazon umiḥya lechol biryotecha
אֲשֶׁר בָּרָאתָ: בָּרוּךְ אַתָּה יְהוָֹה,	asher barata: Baruch atta adonai,
הַזָּן אֶת הַכֹּל: אָמֵן	hazzan et hakkol: Amen:

SATISFY OUR DESIRE, and remove famine from us, and give us our apportioned bread, and set Your table for all. We live and are sustained by virtue of Your patience and Your acts of kindness, and from the opening of Your hand. For You are the One Who feeds, Who provides for, and Who sustains everyone. You even set up sources of food and livelihood for all of the creations which You have created. Blessed are You, Adonai, the One Who feeds everyone. Amen.

End of omition for abbreviated blessing

All continue:

וְעַל הַר־סִינַי יָרַדְתָּ, וְדַבֵּר	Veʿal har Sinai yaradta, vedabber
עִמָּהֶם מִשָּׁמַיִם, וַתִּתֵּן	ʿimmahem mish-shamayim, vattitten
לָהֶם מִשְׁפָּטִים יְשָׁרִים וְתוֹרוֹת	lahem mishpatim yesharim vetorot
אֱמֶת, חֻקִּים וּמִצְוֹת טוֹבִים: וְאֶת־	emet, ḥuḳḳim umitsvot tovim: Veʾet
שַׁבַּת קָדְשְׁךָ הוֹדַעְתָּ לָהֶם	shabbat ḳodshecha hodaʿta lahem,
וּמִצְווֹת וְחֻקִּים וְתוֹרָה, צִוִּיתָ לָהֶם	umitsvot veḥuḳḳim vetora, tsivvita lahem
בְּיַד מֹשֶׁה עַבְדֶּךָ:	beyad Moshé avdecha:

AND YOU CAME DOWN TO MOUNT SINAI, and spoke with them from heaven, and You gave them right ordinances and true laws, commandments, and good statutes; and You made known to them Your holy Sabbath; and You commanded them statutes, commandments, and Torah, by the hand of Moses, Your servant:

כֹּה אָמַר יְהוָה, שִׁמְרוּ מִשְׁפָּט וַעֲשׂוּ
צְדָקָה, כִּי־קְרוֹבָה יְשׁוּעָתִי לָבוֹא
וְצִדְקָתִי לְהִגָּלוֹת: אַשְׁרֵי אֱנוֹשׁ
יַעֲשֶׂה־זֹּאת, וּבֶן־אָדָם יַחֲזִיק בָּהּ,
שֹׁמֵר שַׁבָּת מֵחַלְּלוֹ וְשֹׁמֵר יָדוֹ
מֵעֲשׂוֹת כָּל־רָע:

Ko amar Adonai, shimru mishpat vaʿasu
tsedaḳa, ki ḳerova yeshuʿati lavo
vetsidḳati lehiggalot: Ashré enosh
yaʿasé zot, uven adam yaḥaziḳ bah,
shomer shabbat meḥallelo veshomer yado
meʿasot kol raʿ:

THUS says Adonai: Keep judgement, and do justice; for My salvation is near to come, and My righteousness to be revealed. Blessed is the man who does this, and the son of man who lays hold on it; who keeps the Shabbat and does not profane it, and keeps his hand from doing any evil.

For an abbreviated blessing, omit until the middle of the next page

אִם־תָּשִׁיב מִשַּׁבָּת רַגְלֶךָ, עֲשׂוֹת
חֲפָצֶךָ בְּיוֹם קָדְשִׁי, וְקָרָאתָ
לַשַּׁבָּת עֹנֶג, לִקְדוֹשׁ יְהוָה
מְכֻבָּד, וְכִבַּדְתּוֹ מֵעֲשׂוֹת
דְּרָכֶיךָ, מִמְּצוֹא חֶפְצְךָ,
וְדַבֵּר דָּבָר: אָז תִּתְעַנַּג עַל־יְהוָה,
וְהִרְכַּבְתִּיךָ עַל־בָּמֳתֵי אָרֶץ,
וְהַאֲכַלְתִּיךָ נַחֲלַת יַעֲקֹב אָבִיךָ,
כִּי פִּי יְהוָה דִּבֵּר: אִישׁ אִמּוֹ וְאָבִיו
תִּירָאוּ, וְאֶת־שַׁבְּתֹתַי תִּשְׁמֹרוּ, אֲנִי
יְהוָה אֱלֹהֵיכֶם:

ʾIm tashiv mish-shabbat raḡlecha, ʿasot
ḥafatsecha beyom ḳodshi, veḳarata
lash-shabbat ʿoneḡ, liḳdosh Adonai
mechubbad, vechibbadto meʿasot
derachecha, mimmetso ḥeftsecha,
vedabber davar: Az titʿannaḡ ʿal Adonai,
vehirkavticha ʿal bamoté arets,
vehaʾachalticha naḥalat Yaʿaḳov avicha,
ki pi Adonai dibber: Ish immo veʾaviv
tiraʾu, veʾet shabbetotai tishmoru, ani
Adonai Elohechem:

IF YOU TURN AWAY your foot because of the Shabbat, from pursuing your business on My holy day; and call the Shabbat a delight, and the holy day of Adonai honorable; and you honor it, not doing your wonted ways, nor pursuing your business, nor speaking thereof; then shall you delight yourself in Adonai, and I will make you to ride upon the high places of the earth, and I will feed you with the inheritence of Jacob thy father; for the mouth of Adonai has spoken it. Each person shall revere their mother and father, and shall keep my Shabbatot. I am Adonai, your God.

וַעֲבַדְתֶּם אֵת יְהוָה אֱלֹהֵיכֶם וּבֵרַךְ
אֶת־לַחְמְךָ וְאֶת־מֵימֶיךָ, וַהֲסִרֹתִי
מַחֲלָה מִקִּרְבֶּךָ׃ וּבָתִּים מְלֵאִים
כָּל־טוּב אֲשֶׁר לֹא־מִלֵּאתָ וּבֹרֹת
חֲצוּבִים אֲשֶׁר לֹא־חָצַבְתָּ כְּרָמִים
וְזֵיתִים אֲשֶׁר לֹא־נָטָעְתָּ, וְאָכַלְתָּ
וְשָׂבָעְתָּ׃

Vaʿavadtem et Adonai Elohechem uverach
et laḥmecha veʾet memecha, vahasiroti
maḥala mikkirbecha: Uvattim meleʾim
kol tuv asher lo-milleta uvorot
ḥatsuvim asher lo ḥatsavta keramim
vezetim asher lo-nataʿta, veʾachalta
vesavaʿta.

YOU WILL THEN SERVE Adonai, your God, and He will bless your bread and your water, and I will banish sickness from among you. And houses full of all good things, which you did not fill, and cisterns hewn out, which you did not hew, vineyards and olive-trees, which you did not plant, and you shall eat and be satisfied.

End of abbreviated text

וְאָכַלְתָּ וְשָׂבָעְתָּ, וּבֵרַכְתָּ אֶת־יְהוָה
אֱלֹהֶיךָ עַל־הָאָרֶץ הַטֹּבָה אֲשֶׁר
נָתַן־לָךְ׃

Veʾachalta vesavaʿta, uverachta et Adonai
Elohecha ʿal haʾarets hattova asher
natan lach:

YOU WILL EAT and you will be satisfied, and bless Adonai, your God, for the good land, which He has given you.

בֵּית יִשְׂרָאֵל בָּרְכוּ אֶת־יְהוָה,
★ בָּרוּךְ יהוה׃
בֵּית אַהֲרֹן בָּרְכוּ אֶת־יְהוָה׃
★ בָּרוּךְ יהוה׃

Bet Yisraʾel barechu et Adonai,
★ Baruch Adonai:
Bet Aharon barechu et Adonai,
★ Baruch Adonai:

O HOUSE OF ISRAEL, bless Adonai!
★ Blessed be Adonai!

O HOUSE OF AARON, bless Adonai!
★ Blessed be Adonai!

בֵּית הַלֵּוִי בָּרְכוּ אֶת־יְהוָה,	Bet Hallevi barechu et Adonai,
★ בָּרוּךְ יהוה:	★ Baruch Adonai:
יִרְאֵי יְהוָה בָּרְכוּ אֶת־יְהוָה:	Yiré Adonai barechu et Adonai,
★ בָּרוּךְ יהוה:	★ Baruch Adonai:
בָּרוּךְ יְהוָה ׀ מִצִּיּוֹן שֹׁכֵן	Baruch Adonai mits-tsiyyon shochen
יְרוּשָׁלָםִ	Yerushalayim,
★ הַלְלוּיָהּ:	★ Haleluyah

O HOUSE OF LEVI, bless Adonai!
★ Blessed be Adonai!

O THOSE WHO FEAR ADONAI, bless Adonai!
★ Blessed be Adonai!

BLESSED be Adonai from Zion, He who dwells at Jerusalem!
★ Halleluyah.

For an abbreviated blessing, omit next two pages

כִּי אֱלֹהִים ׀ יוֹשִׁיעַ צִיּוֹן וְיִבְנֶה עָרֵי	Ki Elohim yoshiaʿ tsiyyon veyivné ʿaré
יְהוּדָה וְיָשְׁבוּ שָׁם וִירֵשׁוּהָ:	Yehuda, veyashevu sham vireshuha:
וְזֶרַע עֲבָדָיו יִנְחָלוּהָ וְאֹהֲבֵי שְׁמוֹ	Vezeraʿ ʿavadav yinḥaluha veʾohavé shemo
יִשְׁכְּנוּ־בָהּ: הִנֵּה עֵין יְהוָה אֶל־	yishkenu vah: Hinné ʿen Adonai el
יְרֵאָיו לַמְיַחֲלִים לְחַסְדּוֹ:	yereʾav lamyaḥalim leḥasdo:
לְהַצִּיל מִמָּוֶת נַפְשָׁם	Lehats-tsil mimmavet nafsham,
וּלְחַיּוֹתָם בָּרָעָב: נַפְשֵׁנוּ חִכְּתָה	ulḥayyotam baraʿav: Nafshenu ḥikketa
לַיהוָה עֶזְרֵנוּ וּמָגִנֵּנוּ הוּא:	ladonai ʿezrenu umaḡinnenu hu:

FOR GOD will save Zion, and build the cities of Judah; and they shall abide there, and have it in possession. The seed also of His servants shall inherit it; and they that love His name shall dwell therein. Behold, Adonai's eye is upon those that fear Him, those that hope for his loving kindness. To deliver their soul from death, and to keep them alive in famine. Our soul has waited for Adonai; He is our help and our shield.

כִּי־בוֹ יִשְׂמַח לִבֵּנוּ כִּי בְשֵׁם קָדְשׁוֹ
בָטָחְנוּ: יְהִי־נָא חַסְדְּךָ לְנַחֲמֵנִי
כְּאִמְרָתְךָ לְעַבְדֶּךָ: יְהִי־חַסְדְּךָ
יְהֹוָה עָלֵינוּ כַּאֲשֶׁר יִחַלְנוּ לָךְ:
יְהֹוָה זְכָרָנוּ יְבָרֵךְ יְבָרֵךְ
אֶת־בֵּית יִשְׂרָאֵל יְבָרֵךְ אֶת־בֵּית
אַהֲרֹן: יְבָרֵךְ אֶת הַבַּיִת הַזֶּה
יְבָרֵךְ אֶת בַּעַל הַבַּיִת הַזֶּה יְבָרֵךְ
אֶת הַשֻּׁלְחָן הַזֶּה יְבָרֵךְ אֶת
הַמְסֻבִּין: יְבָרֵךְ יִרְאֵי יְהֹוָה
הַקְּטַנִּים עִם־הַגְּדֹלִים: יֹסֵף
יְהֹוָה עֲלֵיכֶם עֲלֵיכֶם
וְעַל־בְּנֵיכֶם: בְּרוּכִים אַתֶּם לַיהֹוָה
עֹשֵׂה שָׁמַיִם וָאָרֶץ: הַקָּטֹן יִהְיֶה
לָאֶלֶף וְהַצָּעִיר לְגוֹי עָצוּם אֲנִי
יְהֹוָה בְּעִתָּהּ אֲחִישֶׁנָּה:

Ki vo yismaḥ libbenu ki veshem ḳodsho
vataḥnu: Yehi na ḥasdecha lenaḥameni
ke'imratecha le'avdecha: Yehi ḥasdecha
Adonai 'alenu ka'asher yiḥalnu lach:
Adonai zecharanu yevarech, yevarech
et bet Yisra'el, yevarech et bet
Aharon: Yevarech et habbayit hazzé,
yevarech et ba'al habbayit hazzé, yevarech
et hash-shulḥan hazzé, yevarech et
hamesubin: Yevarech yiré Adonai
haḳḳetannim 'im haggedolim: Yosef
Adonai 'alechem, 'alechem
ve'al benechem: beruchim attem ladonai
'osé shamayim va'arets: Haḳḳaton yihyé
la'elef vehats-tsa'ir leğoy 'atsum ani
Adonai be'ittah aḥishenna:

FOR IN HIM *does our heart rejoice, because we have trusted in His holy name. Let Your mercy give me consolation, in accordance with Your utterance to Your servant. Let Your mercy, Adonai, be upon us, according as we have waited for You. Adonai has been mindful of us. May He bless – May He bless the house of Israel; He will bless the house of Aaron. May He bless this home, may He bless this homeowner, may He bless this table, and may He bless those who sit around it. He will bless them that fear Adonai, both small and great. May Adonai increase you more and more, you and your children. Blessed be you of Adonai who made heaven and earth. The smallest shall become a thousand, and the least a mighty nation; I, Adonai, will hasten it in its time.*

יְהֹוָה יֵחַתּוּ מְרִיבָו עָלָו
בַּשָּׁמַיִם יַרְעֵם יְהֹוָה יָדִין אַפְסֵי־
אָרֶץ וְיִתֶּן־עֹז לְמַלְכּוֹ וְיָרֵם קֶרֶן
מְשִׁיחוֹ:

Adonai yeḥattu merivav ʿalav
bash-shamayim yarʿem Adonai yadin afsé
arets veyitten ʿoz lemalko, veyarem ḳeren
meshiḥo:

THEY THAT STRIVE WITH ADONAI shall be broken to pieces; against them will He thunder in heaven; Adonai will judge the ends of the earth; and He will give strength unto His king, and exalt the horn of His anointed.

מַגְדִּיל יְשׁוּעוֹת מַלְכּוֹ וְעֹשֶׂה חֶסֶד ׀
לִמְשִׁיחוֹ לְדָוִד וּלְזַרְעוֹ עַד־עוֹלָם:
בּוֹנֵה יְרוּשָׁלַיִם יְהֹוָה נִדְחֵי יִשְׂרָאֵל
יְכַנֵּס: בּוֹרֵא נִיב שְׂפָתָיִם שָׁלוֹם ׀
שָׁלוֹם לָרָחוֹק וְלַקָּרוֹב אָמַר יְהֹוָה
וּרְפָאתִיו: הַמְשֵׁל וָפַחַד עִמּוֹ עֹשֶׂה
שָׁלוֹם בִּמְרוֹמָיו:

Maḡdil yeshuʿot malko veʿosé ḥesed
limshiḥo leDavid ulzarʿo ʿad ʿolam:
Boné Yerushalayim Adonai nidḥé Yisraʾel
yechannes: Boré niv sefatayim, shalom
shalom laraḥoḳ velaḳḳarov amar Adonai
urfativ: Hamshel vafaḥad ʿimmo ʿosé
shalom bimromav:

HE GIVES GREAT SALVATION to His king; and shows mercy to His anointed, to David and to his seed, forevermore. Adonai builds up Jerusalem; He gathers together the dispersed of Israel. Peace, peace, to him that is far off and to him that is near, said Adonai, Who creates the fruit of the lips; and I will heal him. Dominion and fear are with Him; He makes peace in His high places.

End of abbreviated text

יְהֹוָה עֹז לְעַמּוֹ יִתֵּן,
* יְהֹוָה ׀ יְבָרֵךְ אֶת־עַמּוֹ בַשָּׁלוֹם:
בָּרוּךְ יְהֹוָה לְעוֹלָם,
* אָמֵן ׀ וְאָמֵן:

Adonai ʿoz leʿammo yitten,
* Adonai yevarech et ʿammo vash-shalom:
Baruch Adonai leʿolam,
* Amen veʾamen:

ADONAI will give strength to His people;
Adonai will bless His people with peace.

BLESSED be Adonai forevermore;
Amen, and Amen.

Songs for Shabbat

זמירות שבת

YATSAR HA'EL

by Rav Ya'aḳov

יָצַר הָאֵל אֶת הָעוֹלָם:	Yatsar ha'El et ha'olam:
שֵׁשֶׁת יָמִים כִּלָּה כֻּלָּם:	Sheshet yamim killa chullam:
יוֹם שְׁבִיעִי מִכְּלָלָם:	Yom shevi'i mikkelalam:
קִדֵּשׁ אוֹתוֹ גַּם בֵּרְכָהוּ:	Ḳiddesh oto gam berchahu:
★ יצר האל...	★ YATSAR HA'EL...
עַל כֵּן צִוָּה לִבְנֵי עַמּוֹ:	'Al ken tsivva livné 'ammo:
לִשְׁבּוֹת בַּיּוֹם הַהוּא לִשְׁמוֹ:	Lishbot bayyom hahu lishmo:
וּלְהִשְׁתַּחֲווֹת אֶל הֲדוֹמוֹ:	Ulhishtaḥavot el hadomo:
עִם שְׁבָחוֹת שַׁבְּחוּהוּ:	'Im shevaḥot shabbeḥuhu:
★ יצר האל...	★ YATSAR HA'EL...

GOD CREATED the world.
In six days, He finished all.
The seventh day from all of them –
He declared it holy and He blessed it.

★ *GOD CREATED . . .*

Therefore, He commanded His people,
To cease work on this day for the sake of His name,
And to bow down toward His footstool,
Praise Him with praises!

★ *GOD CREATED . . .*

קִרְאוּ שִׁירִים בַּנְּעִימִים:	Ḳiru shirim banneʿimim:
וּשְׁתוּ יֵינוֹת עִם מַטְעִימִים:	Ushtu yenot ʿim matʿimim:
יַעַן זֶה יוֹם תַּעֲצוּמִים:	Yaʿan zé yom taʿatsumim:
כִּי קָדוֹשׁ הוּא קַדְּשׁוּהוּ:	Ki ḳadosh hu ḳaddeshuhu:
★ יצר האל...	★ YATSAR HA'EL . . .
בֵּרַךְ הָאֵל אֶת הַשַּׁבָּת:	Berach ha'El et hash-shabbat:
יַעַן כִּי בוֹ בְּיוֹם שָׁבַת:	Yaʿan ki vo beyom shavat:
מוֹרֶה אֶל קַדְמוּתוֹ שַׁבָּת:	Moré el ḳadmuto shabbat:
כִּי אֶחָד הוּא יַחֲדוּהוּ:	Ki eḥad hu yaḥaduhu:
★ יצר האל...	★ YATSAR HA'EL . . .

Sing songs with tunes,
And drink wines with savory food,
Because it is a mighty day.
It is a holy day – declare it holy.

★ *GOD CREATED . . .*

God blessed the Shabbat,
For on this day, He ceased work.
Shabbat indicates His ancientness.
He is one – Know He is one.

★ *GOD CREATED . . .*

YAH ZIMRATI

by Rav Yehuda

יָהּ זִמְרָתִי צִוָּה אֶתְכֶם:	Yah zimrati tsivva etchem:
אִישׁ יִשְׂרָאֵל בִּמְנוּחַתְכֶם:	Ish Yisra'el bimnuḥatchem:
יוֹם הַשַּׁבָּת שִׁמְרוּ לָכֶם:	Yom hash-shabbat shimru lachem:
אוֹת הִיא בֵּינִי וּבֵינֵיכֶם:	Ot hi beni uvenechem:
★ יה זמרתי	★ YAH ZIMRATI . . .
הוּא יוֹם קָדוֹשׁ מִן הַיָּמִים:	Hu yom ḳadosh min hayyamim:
אוֹר הַגָּנוּז סוֹד לַתְּמִימִים:	Or hagganuz sod lattemimim:
רֶמֶז גָּדוֹל רֵיחַ סַמִּים:	Remez gadol re'aḥ sammim:
חֻקַּת עוֹלָם לְדוֹרוֹתֵיכֶם:	Ḥuḳḳat 'olam ledorotechem:
★ יה זמרתי...	★ Yah Zimrati . . .

YAH, MY PRAISE, commanded you,
Each Israelite, to rest.
Keep the Shabbat day.
It is a sign between God and you.

★ *YAH, MY PRAISE . . .*

It is the holiest day of the week.
It is a hidden light, a secret for the honest people,
A great sign, a smell of sweet spices,
And an eternal statute for your generations.

★ *YAH, MY PRAISE . . .*

וּרְאוּ וּדְעוּ שַׁבָּת קֹדֶשׁ:	Uru udʿu shabbat ḳodesh:
יוֹם כִּפּוּרִים הוּא לַחֹדֶשׁ:	Yom kippurim hu laḥodesh:
וּשְׁנַת שֶׁבַע גַּם הִיא חֹפֶשׁ:	Ushnat shevaʿ gam hi ḥofesh:
הִיא חָכְמַתְכֶם וּבִינַתְכֶם:	Hi ḥochmatchem uvinatchem:
★ יה זמרתי...	★ YAH ZIMRATI . . .
דִּשְׁנֵי אֶרֶץ הֵכִין אָיוֹם:	Dishné erets hechin ayom:
לָהֶם מִשְׁנֵה טֶרֶף יוֹם יוֹם:	Lahem mishné teref yom yom:
אִכְלוּ הָעָם שַׁבָּת הַיּוֹם:	Ichlu haʿam shabbat hayyom:
כִּי קֹדֶשׁ הוּא יִהְיֶה לָכֶם:	Ki ḳodesh hu yihyé lachem:
★ יה זמרתי...	★ YAH ZIMRATI . . .

And see and know – Shabbat is holy,
Like the Day of Atonement of the [Seventh] month.
And the seventh year is also freedom.
This is your wisdom and your understanding.

★ *YAH, MY PRAISE . . .*

The great God made posterity.
He gave them twice as much food as usual.
People, eat; it is Shabbat,
Because it shall be holy to you.

★ *YAH, MY PRAISE . . .*

הַלֶּחֶם הוּא מִשָּׁמַיִם:	Halleḥem hu mish-shamayim:
צֵדָה שָׁלַח אֶל הַחַיִּים:	Tseda shalaḥ el haḥayyim:
גַּם לֹא הִבְאִישׁ זֶה יוֹמַיִם:	Gam lo hivish zé yomayim:
לְמַעַן יֵדְעוּ דוֹרוֹתֵיכֶם:	Lemaʿan yedeʿu dorotechem:
★ יה זמרתי...	★ YAH ZIMRATI . . .

The bread was from heaven.
God sent provisions to the people.
It didn't spoil for two days,
To let your generations know.

★ *YAH, MY PRAISE . . .*

MATOḲ DEVAR TORA

By Rav Moshé

מָתוֹק דְּבַר תּוֹרָה:	Matoḳ devar tora:
מִמָּן בְּפִי וּדְבָשׁ:	Mimman befi udvash:
עַל כֵּן אֲנִי אָשִׁיר:	ʿal ken ani ashir:
לָאֵל בְּשִׁיר חָדָשׁ:	La'El beshir ḥadash:
★ מתוק דבר תורה...	★ MATOḲ DEVAR TORA...
שֵׁשֶׁת יְמֵי מַעֲשֶׂה:	Sheshet yemé maʿsé:
בָּם כָּל יְצוּר נִבְרָא:	Bam kol yetsur nivra:
וּבְיוֹם שְׁבִיעִי בוֹ:	Uvyom sheviʿi vo:
שָׁבַת וַיִּנָּפַשׁ:	Shavat vayyinnafash:
★ מתוק דבר תורה...	★ MATOḲ DEVAR TORA...

THE WORD OF TORAH IS SWEETER
Than manna in my mouth or honey.
So I will sing
To God a new song.

★ *THE WORD OF TORAH IS SWEETER...*

The six days of work –
Every creature was created in them.
And on the seventh day,
God ceased work and rested.

★ *THE WORD OF TORAH IS SWEETER...*

הָחֵשׁ פְּדוּת עַמָּךְ:	Haḥesh pedut ʿammach:
כִּי רַב מְאֹד עִמָּךְ:	Ki rav meʾod ʿimmach:
הָאוֹמְרִים תָּמִיד:	Haʾomerim tamid:
יִגְדַּל וְיִתְקַדָּשׁ:	Yiḡdal veyitḳaddash:
★ מתוק דבר תורה...	★ MATOḲ DEVAR TORA...

Hasten the deliverance of Your people,
For it is very great with You.
The people who always say,
"[May Your name] grow and be sanctified."

★ *THE WORD OF TORAH IS SWEETER...*

Havdala for After Shabbat

הבדלה למוצאי שבת

HAVDALA

Raise a cup of wine:

כּוֹס־יְשׁוּעוֹת אֶשָּׂא, וּבְשֵׁם יְהֹוָה
אֶקְרָא: אָנָּא יְהֹוָה הוֹשִׁיעָה נָּא,
★ אָנָּא יְהֹוָה הַצְלִיחָה נָּא:

בָּרוּךְ הַבָּא בְּשֵׁם יְהֹוָה,
בֵּרַכְנוּכֶם מִבֵּית יְהֹוָה: אֵל ׀ יְהֹוָה
וַיָּאֶר לָנוּ, אִסְרוּ־חַג בַּעֲבֹתִים,
★ עַד־קַרְנוֹת הַמִּזְבֵּחַ:

אֱלֹהִים יְחָנֵּנוּ וִיבָרְכֵנוּ, יָאֵר
פָּנָיו אִתָּנוּ סֶלָה: הָבָה־לָּנוּ עֶזְרַת
מִצָּר, וְשָׁוְא תְּשׁוּעַת אָדָם:
בֵּאלֹהִים נַעֲשֶׂה־חָיִל, וְהוּא יָבוּס
צָרֵינוּ: בֵּאלֹהִים נַעֲשֶׂה־חָיִל, וְהוּא
יָבוּס אוֹיְבֵינוּ: בֵּאלֹהִים הִלַּלְנוּ כָל־
הַיּוֹם,
★ וְשִׁמְךָ ׀ לְעוֹלָם נוֹדֶה סֶלָה:

Kos yeshuʿot essa, uvshem Adonai
eḳra: Anna Adonai hoshiʿa na,
★ Anna Adonai hatsliḥa na:

Baruch habba beshem Adonai,
berachnuchem mibbet Adonai: El Adonai
vayyaʾer lanu, isru ḥag̅ baʿavotim,
★ ʿad ḳarnot hammizbeʾaḥ:

Elohim yeḥonnenu vivarechenu, yaʾer
panav ittanu sela: Hava lanu ʿezrat
mits-tsar, veshav teshuʿat adam:
Belohim naʿasé ḥayil, vehu yavus
tsarenu: Belohim naʿasé ḥayil vehu
yavus oyevenu: Belohim hillalnu chol
hayyom,
★ Veshimcha leʿolam nodé sela:

I WILL LIFT UP THE CUP OF SALVATION, and call upon the name of Adonai. O Adonai, deliver us!
★ O Adonai, let us prosper!

BLESSED is he who comes in the name of Adonai; we have blessed you from the house of Adonai. God is Adonai, Who has shown us light;
★ Bind the sacrifice with cords to the horns of the altar.

GOD be gracious to us, and bless us; let His face shine upon us; Selah: Give us help against the enemy, for vain is the help of man. Through God, we shall do valiantly, for He will tread down our enemies. Through God, we shall do valiantly, for He will tread down our adversaries. In God, we have gloried all day long,
★ And we praise Your name forever; Selah.

בֵּאלֹהִים אֲהַלֵּל דָּבָר בַּיהוָה אֲהַלֵּל
דָּבָר: בֵּאלֹהִים אֲהַלֵּל דְּבָרוֹ,
בֵּאלֹהִים בָּטַחְתִּי לֹא אִירָא, מַה־
יַּעֲשֶׂה בָשָׂר לִי: בֵּאלֹהִים בָּטַחְתִּי
לֹא אִירָא, מַה־יַּעֲשֶׂה אָדָם לִי:
יְהוָה לִי לֹא אִירָא, מַה־יַּעֲשֶׂה לִי
אָדָם: יְהוָה לִי בְּעֹזְרָי, וַאֲנִי אֶרְאֶה
בְשֹׂנְאָי: טוֹב לַחֲסוֹת בַּיהוָה,
מִבְּטֹחַ בָּאָדָם: טוֹב לַחֲסוֹת
בַּיהוָה, מִבְּטֹחַ בִּנְדִיבִים:
אַל־תִּבְטְחוּ בִנְדִיבִים,
* בְּבֶן־אָדָם ׀ שֶׁאֵין לוֹ תְשׁוּעָה:

Belohim ahallel davar badonai ahallel
davar: Belohim ahallel devaro,
Belohim bataḥti lo ira, ma
ya‘asé vasar li: Belohim bataḥti
lo ira, ma ya‘asé adam li:
Adonai li lo ira, ma ya‘asé li
adam: Adonai li be‘ozerai, va’ani eré
vesone’ai: Tov laḥasot badonai,
mibbetoaḥ ba’adam: Tov laḥasot
badonai, mibbetoaḥ bindivim:
Al tivteḥu vindivim,
* Beven adam she’en lo teshu‘a:

IN GOD, Whose word I praise; in Adonai, Whose word I praise. In God, Whose word I praise; in God, I have put my trust; I will not fear: what can flesh do to me? In God, I have put my trust; I will not be afraid: what can man do to me? Adonai is on my side; I will not fear: what can man do to me? Adonai takes my part with those who help me; therefore, I shall gaze upon those who hate me. It is better to take refuge in Adonai than to put confidence in man. It is better to take refuge in Adonai than to put confidence in generous people. Do not put your trust in generous people,

* *nor in the son of man, in whom there is no help.*

בָּרוּךְ אַתָּה יְהֹוָה אֱלֹהֵינוּ מֶלֶךְ
הָעוֹלָם, הַמַּבְדִּיל בֵּין קֹדֶשׁ לְחֹל,
בֵּין אוֹר לְחֹשֶׁךְ, בֵּין יִשְׂרָאֵל
לָעַמִּים הַפְּרָאִים, בֵּין טָמֵא
לְטָהוֹר, בֵּין שֵׁשֶׁת יְמֵי הַמַּעֲשֶׂה
לְיוֹם הַשְּׁבִיעִי: כַּכָּתוּב, וִהְיִיתֶם לִי
קְדֹשִׁים כִּי קָדוֹשׁ אֲנִי יְהֹוָה, וָאַבְדִּל
אֶתְכֶם מִן־הָעַמִּים לִהְיוֹת לִי:
וְכָתוּב, וּלְהַבְדִּיל בֵּין הַקֹּדֶשׁ וּבֵין
הַחֹל, וּבֵין הַטָּמֵא וּבֵין הַטָּהוֹר:
וּלְהוֹרֹת אֶת־בְּנֵי יִשְׂרָאֵל, אֵת כָּל-
הַחֻקִּים אֲשֶׁר דִּבֶּר יְהֹוָה אֲלֵיהֶם
★ בְּיַד־מֹשֶׁה:

Baruch atta Adonai Elohenu melech
haʿolam, hammavdil ben ḳodesh leḥol,
ben or leḥoshech, ben Yisraʾel
laʿammim happeraʾim, ben tamé
letahor, ben sheshet yemé hammaʿasé
leyom hash-sheviʿi: Kakkatuv, vihyitem li
ḳedoshim ki ḳadosh ani Adonai, vaʾavdil
etchem min haʿammim lihyot li:
Vechatuv, ulhavdil ben haḳḳodesh uven
haḥol, uven hattamé uven hattahor:
Ulhorot et bené Yisraʾel, et kol
haḥuḳḳim asher dibber Adonai alehem,
★ Beyad Moshé:

BLESSED are You, Adonai, our God, King of the universe, Who creates a difference between the holy and the common, between the light and darkness, between Israel and the wild nations, between the impure and the pure, between the six workdays and the seventh day. As it is written: And ye shall be holy unto Me; for I, Adonai, am holy; and I have separated you from the peoples to become Mine. And it is written: And that you may differentiate between the holy and common, and between the impure and the pure. And that you may teach the children of Israel all the statutes, which Adonai has spoken to them
★ *by the hand of Moses.*

אֱלֹהֵינוּ וֵאלֹהֵי אֲבוֹתֵינוּ, הָחֵל	Elohenu velohé avotenu, haḥel
עָלֵינוּ שֵׁשֶׁת יְמֵי הַמַּעֲשֶׂה הַבָּאִים	ʿalenu sheshet yemé hammaʿasé habbaʾim
לִקְרָאתֵנוּ לְשָׁלוֹם וּלְשַׁלְוָה,	liḳratenu leshalom ulshalva,
לְשָׂשׂוֹן וּלְשִׂמְחָה, לִישׁוּעָה	lesason ulsimḥa, lishuʿa
וּלְנֶחָמָה, לְפַרְנָסָה וּלְכַלְכָּלָה:	ulneḥama, lefarnasa ulchalkala:
חֲשׂוּכִים מִכָּל דָּבָר רָע, וּמֻצָּלִים	Ḥasuchim mikkol davar raʿ, umuts-tsalim
מִכָּל חֵטְא וְעָוֹן וַעֲבֵירָה:	mikkol ḥet veʿavon vaʿavera:
וּמֻדְבָּקִים בְּלִמּוּד וְהֶגְיוֹן	Umudbaḳim belimmud veheḡyon
תּוֹרָתֶךָ, וַחֲנוּנִים מֵאִתְּךָ	toratecha, vaḥanunim meʾittecha
חָכְמָה דֵּעָה	ḥochma deʿa,
★ וְהַשְׂכֵּל וּבִינָה:	★ Vehaskel uvina:

OUR GOD AND GOD OF OUR ANCESTORS, *make the following six workdays be calm and safe days, happy and joyous days, days of salvation and relief, and days of maintaining and supporting; spared of all evil things and saved from all sin, offense, and crime. Make them days of studying Your Torah, and graced with wisdom, knowledge,*
★ *education, and understanding.*

וְלֹא קִנְאָתֵנוּ וְשִׂנְאָתֵנוּ תַּעֲלֶה עַל	Velo ḳinatenu vesinatenu taʿalé ʿal
לֵב אָדָם: וְלֹא קִנְאַת וְשִׂנְאַת אָדָם	lev adam: Velo ḳinat vesinat adam
תַּעֲלֶה עַל לִבֵּנוּ: וְכָל הַיּוֹעֵץ עָלֵינוּ	taʿalé ʿal libbenu: Vechol hayyoʿets ʿalenu
עֵצָה טוֹבָה וּמַחֲשָׁבָה טוֹבָה קַיְּמֵהוּ	ʿetsa tova umaḥashava tova ḳayyemehu
וְקַיֵּם עֲצָתוֹ: כָּאָמוּר, וְחַנֹּתִי אֶת־	veḳayyem ʿatsato: Kaʾamur, veḥannoti et
אֲשֶׁר אָחֹן,	asher aḥon,
★ וְרִחַמְתִּי אֶת־אֲשֶׁר אֲרַחֵם:	★ Veriḥamti et asher araḥem:

AND DO NOT *let any person be jealous of us or hate us. And do not let us be jealous of any person or hate them. And fulfill any good counsel or good thought that any person thinks about us. As it is written: And I will be gracious to whom I will be gracious,*
★ *and I will show mercy on whom I will show mercy.*

וְכָל הַיּוֹעֵץ עָלֵינוּ עֵצָה רָעָה
וּמַחֲשָׁבָה רָעָה, קַלְקֵל מַחֲשַׁבְתּוֹ,
הָפֵר עֲצָתוֹ: כָּאָמוּר עֻצוּ עֵצָה
וְתֻפָר, דַּבְּרוּ דָבָר וְלֹא יָקוּם
★ כִּי עִמָּנוּ אֵל:

Vechol hayoʿets ʿalenu ʿetsa raʿa
umaḥashava raʿa, ḳalḳel maḥashavto,
hafer ʿatsato: Kaʾamur ʿutsu ʿetsa
vetufar, dabberu davar velo yaḳum
★ Ki ʿimmanu El:

רַבּוֹת מַחֲשָׁבוֹת בְּלֶב־אִישׁ, וַעֲצַת
יְהוָה הִיא תָקוּם: כִּי־יְהוָה צְבָאוֹת
יָעָץ וּמִי יָפֵר,
★ וְיָדוֹ הַנְּטוּיָה וּמִי יְשִׁיבֶנָּה:

Rabbot maḥashavot belev ish, vaʿatsat
Adonai hi taḳum: Ki Adonai Tsevaʾot
yaʿats umi yafer,
★ Veyado hannetuya umi yeshivenna:

בָּרוּךְ אַתָּה יְהוָה אֱלֹהֵינוּ מֶלֶךְ
הָעוֹלָם, הַמֵּפֵר עֵצוֹת הָרָעוֹת
הַמִּתְרַגְּשׁוֹת הַמִּתְלַחֲשׁוֹת
מֵעָלֵינוּ, וּמֵעַל בָּתֵּינוּ וּמֵעַל כָּל בָּתֵּי
כְּלַל עַמְּךָ בֵּית יִשְׂרָאֵל:
★ אָמֵן:

Baruch atta Adonai Elohenu melech
haʿolam, hammefer ʿetsot haraʿot
hammitraggeshot hammitlaḥashot
meʿalenu, umeʿal battenu umeʿal kol batté
kelal ʿammecha bet Yisraʾel:
★ Amen:

AND MAKE *any bad counsel or bad thought that any person thinks about us come to nothing. As it is written: Take counsel together, and it shall come to nothing; speak the word, and it shall not stand;*
★ *for God is with us.*

THERE ARE MANY *plans in a man's heart; nevertheless, the counsel of Adonai shall stand. For Adonai of hosts has planned, and who will annul it?*
★ *And His hand is stretched out, and who shall turn it back?*

BLESSED *are You, Adonai, our God, King of the universe, Who brings the thoughts of bad counsel about us, our houses, and on the houses of all Your people, Israel, to nothing.*
★ *Amen.*

וּבָרוּךְ אֱלֹהֵינוּ מֶלֶךְ	Uvaruch Elohenu melech
הָעוֹלָם הַמַּבְדִּיל בֵּין קֹדֶשׁ לְחוֹל,	ha῾olam hammavdil ben ḳodesh leḥol,
וְהַנּוֹתֵן לָנוּ שָׂשׂוֹן וְשִׂמְחָה וּבוֹרֵא	vehannoten lanu sason vesimḥa uvoré
פְּרִי הַגָּפֶן:	peri haggafen:
★ אָמֵן:	★ Amen:

BLESSED are You, Adonai, our God, King of the universe, Who creates a difference between the holy and the common and gives us joy and happiness, and Who creates the fruit of the vine.
★ *Amen.*

And then say the blessing over the perfume spices:

בָּרוּךְ אַתָּה יְהוָֹה אֱלֹהֵינוּ מֶלֶךְ	Baruch atta Adonai Elohenu melech
הָעוֹלָם בּוֹרֵא מִינֵי	ha῾olam boré miné
ואם מקורו בעשב תאמר: עִשְׂבֵי	*for plants or herbs, say:* ῾isbé
ואם מקורו בעץ תאמר: עֲצֵי	*for trees, say:* ῾atsé
בְשָׂמִים.	besamim:
★ אָמֵן:	★ Amen

BLESSED are You, Adonai, our God, King of the universe,
Who creates various types of fragrance
for plants or herbs, say: fragrant plants;
for trees, say: fragrant trees.
★ *Amen*

A Song for Havdala
זמר להבדלה

☙ ET KOS YESHUʿOT

by Rav Elyakim

אֶת כּוֹס יְשׁוּעוֹת: אֶשָּׂא בִּזִמְרָה:	Et kos yeshuʿot: Essa bezimra:
וּבְשֵׁם יְהֹוָה: אוֹדֶה וְאֶקְרָא:	Uvshem Adonai: Odé veʾeḳra:
★ את כוס ישועות...	★ ET KOS YESHUʿOT . . .
לַיְלָה וְיוֹמָם: עֻזּוֹ אֲמַלֵּל:	Layla veyomạm: ʿUzzo amallel:
וּלְשֵׁם כְּבוֹדוֹ: תָּמִיד אֲהַלֵּל:	Ulshem kevodo: Tamid ahallel:
כִּי הוּא לְבַדּוֹ: יוֹצֵר מְחוֹלֵל:	Ki hu levaddo: Yotser meḥolel:
מַעְלָה וּמַטָּה: יָצַר וּבָרָא:	Maʿla umatta: Yatsar uvara:
★ את כוס ישועות...	★ ET KOS YESHUʿOT . . .
יָרוּם וְיִגְדַּל: עַל כָּל יְצוּרִים:	Yarum veyiḡdal: ʿAl kol yetsurim:
זִכְרוֹ מְבוֹרָךְ: נֶצַח לְדוֹרִים:	Zichro mevorach: Netsaḥ ledorim:
מוֹרִישׁ וּמַעֲשִׁיר: מַשְׁפִּיל וּמֵרִים:	Morish umaʿshir: Mashpil umerim:
לוֹ הַגְּדֻלָּה: לוֹ הַגְּבוּרָה:	Lo haggedulla: Lo haggevura:
★ את כוס ישועות...	★ ET KOS YESHUʿOT . . .

I WILL LIFT UP THE CUP OF SALVATION, while I am singing,
And I call upon the name of Adonai, and thank Him.

★ *I WILL LIFT UP . . .*

All day and night, I will proclaim His glory.
And His honorable name, I will always praise,
Because He is the sole creator.
He created heavens and earth.

★ *I WILL LIFT UP . . .*

May His name grow and rise up upon all creatures.
His memory is blessed, a sign forever.
He makes people poor and rich, low and high.
He has the greatness, He has the might.

★ *I WILL LIFT UP . . .*

קָרוֹב יְהֹוָה: תָּמִיד לְקוֹרְאָיו:	Ḳarov Adonai: Tamid leḳoreʾav:
רַבּוּ וְעָצְמוּ: נִסֵּי פְלָאָיו:	Rabbu veʿatsemu: Nissé felaʾav:
טוּבוֹ וְרַחֲמָיו: עַל כָּל בְּרוּאָיו:	Tuvo veraḥamav: ʿAl kol beruʾav:
לָכֵן בְּצָרוֹת: נִמְצָא לְעֶזְרָה:	Lachen betsarot: Nimtsa leʿezra:
★ את כוס ישועות...	★ ET KOS YESHUʿOT . . .
יְקָרוּ דְרָכָיו: עַל כָּל דְּרָכִים:	Yaḳeru derachav: ʿAl kol derachim:
מַנְהִיג וּמוֹשֵׁל: עַל כָּל פְּלָכִים:	Manhiḡ umoshel: ʿAl kol pelachim:
נוֹרָא וְעֶלְיוֹן: מֶלֶךְ מְלָכִים:	Nora veʿelyon: Melech melachim:
אַדִּיר וְגָדוֹל: גִּבּוֹר וְנוֹרָא:	Addir veḡadol: Gibbor venora:
★ את כוס ישועות...	★ ET KOS YESHUʿOT . . .

Adonai is always close to His callers.
His miraculous wonders are many and powerful.
His kindness and mercy are upon all His creatures.
Therefore, He can always help with all troubles.

★ *I WILL LIFT UP . . .*

His ways are more precious than other ways.
He is the leader and ruler of all the districts.
He is awesome and superior, King of kings,
Mighty and great, tremendous and awesome.

★ *I WILL LIFT UP . . .*

מָעוֹז וּמַחְסֶה: אֶל דַל וְאֶבְיוֹן:	Maʿoz umaḥsé: El dal ve'evyon:
יִשְׁלַח לְעַמּוֹ: יֶשַׁע וּפִדְיוֹן:	Yishlaḥ leʿammo: Yeshaʿ ufidyon:
מֶלֶךְ וְכֹהֵן: יָבִיא לְצִיּוֹן:	Melech vechohen: Yavi letsiyyon:
יִבְנֶה מְהֵרָה: בֵּית הַבְּחִירָה:	Yivné mehera: Bet habbeḥira:
* את כוס ישועות...	* Et kos yeshuʿot . . .

He is like a fortress and a shelter to the poor and wretched.
He will send to His people salvation and redemption.
He will bring to Zion king and priest.
He will build soon the Holy Temple.

* *I WILL LIFT UP . . .*

Blessings for Every Day

ברכות לכל יום ויום

A BEDTIME PRAYER

בָּרוּךְ אַתָּה יְהוָה אֱלֹהֵינוּ מֶלֶךְ
הָעוֹלָם, הַמַּפִּיל חֶבְלֵי שֵׁנָה עַל
עֵינָי, וּתְנוּמָה עַל עַפְעַפָּי. יְהִי רָצוֹן
מִלְּפָנֶיךָ יְהוָה אֱלֹהַי וֵאלֹהֵי אֲבוֹתַי
שֶׁתַּשְׁכִּיבֵנִי לְשָׁלוֹם, וְתַעֲמִידֵנִי
מִמִּטָּתִי לְחַיִּים וּלְשָׁלוֹם, וְאַל
יְבַהֲלוּנִי חֲלוֹמוֹת רָעִים וְהִרְהוּרִים
רָעִים. בָּרוּךְ אַתָּה יְהוָה, הַמֵּאִיר
לָעוֹלָם כֻּלּוֹ בִּכְבוֹדוֹ:

Baruch atta Adonai Elohenu melech
haʿolam, hammappil ḥevlé shena ʿal
ʿenai, utnuma ʿal ʿafʿappai. Yehi ratson
millefanecha Adonai Elohai velohé avotai
shettashkiveni leshalom, vetaʿamideni
mimmittati leḥayyim ulshalom, veʾal
yevahaluni ḥalomot raʿim vehirhurim
raʿim. Baruch atta Adonai, hammeʾir
laʿolam kullo bichvodo:

שְׁמַע יִשְׂרָאֵל, יְהוָה אֱלֹהֵינוּ
יְהוָה ׀ אֶחָד: אֶחָד אֱלֹהֵינוּ, גָּדוֹל
אֲדֹנֵינוּ, קָדוֹשׁ וְנוֹרָא שְׁמוֹ
לְעוֹלָם וָעֶד:

Shemaʿ Yisraʾel, Adonai Elohenu
Adonai Eḥad: eḥad Elohenu, gadol
Adonenu, ḳadosh venora shemo
leʿolam vaʿed:

BLESSED *are You, Adonai, our God, King of the universe, Who lays the bands of sleep upon my eyes, and slumber upon my eyelids. May it be Your will, Adonai, my God and the God of my fathers, that I lie down in peace and rise up again, alive and in peace. And that I will not have any bad dreams or bad thoughts. Blessed are You, Adonai, Who gives light to the whole universe in your glory.*

HEAR, O ISRAEL*: Adonai is our God; Adonai is one. One is our God, great is our Lord, holy and awesome is His name, forever and ever.*

וְאָהַבְתָּ אֵת יְהוָה אֱלֹהֶיךָ,
בְּכָל־לְבָבְךָ וּבְכָל־נַפְשְׁךָ
וּבְכָל־מְאֹדֶךָ: וְהָיוּ הַדְּבָרִים
הָאֵלֶּה, אֲשֶׁר אָנֹכִי מְצַוְּךָ הַיּוֹם
עַל־לְבָבֶךָ: וְשִׁנַּנְתָּם לְבָנֶיךָ
וְדִבַּרְתָּ בָּם, בְּשִׁבְתְּךָ בְּבֵיתֶךָ
וּבְלֶכְתְּךָ בַדֶּרֶךְ וּבְשָׁכְבְּךָ
וּבְקוּמֶךָ: וּקְשַׁרְתָּם לְאוֹת עַל־יָדֶךָ,
וְהָיוּ לְטֹטָפֹת בֵּין עֵינֶיךָ: וּכְתַבְתָּם
עַל־מְזֻזוֹת בֵּיתֶךָ וּבִשְׁעָרֶיךָ: בָּרוּךְ
יְהוָה לְעוֹלָם, אָמֵן | וְאָמֵן:

Ve'ahavta et Adonai Elohecha,
bechol levavecha uvchol nafshecha
uvchol me'odecha: Vehayu haddevarim
ha'ellé, asher anochi metsavvecha hayyom
ʿal levavecha: Veshinnantam levanecha
vedibbarta bam, beshivtecha bevetecha
uvlechtecha vadderech uvshochbecha
uvḳumecha: Uḳshartam le'ot ʿal yadecha,
vehayu letotafot ben ʿenecha: Uchtavtam
ʿal mezuzot betecha uvishʿarecha: Baruch
Adonai leʿolam, Amen ve'amen:

AND YOU SHALL LOVE Adonai your God with all your heart, and with all your soul, and with all your might. Take to heart these instructions with which I charge you this day. You shall teach them diligently to your children and shall talk of them when you sit in your house and when you walk by the way and when you lie down and when you rise up. Bind them as a sign on your hand, and they shall be as a remembrance between your eyes. Write them on the door-posts of your house and on your gates. Blessed be Adonai forevermore; Amen, and Amen.

A PRAYER AFTER WAKING UP

(For Males)

מוֹדֶה אֲנִי לְפָנֶיךָ מֶלֶךְ חַי וְקַיָּם	Modé ani lefanecha melech ḥai veḳayyam
שֶׁהֶחֱזַרְתָּ בִּי נִשְׁמָתִי בְּחֶמְלָה,	sheheḥezarta bi nishmati beḥemla,
רַבָּה אֱמוּנָתֶךָ: אֱלֹהַי, נְשָׁמָה	rabba emunatecha: Elohai, neshama
שֶׁנָּתַתָּ בִּי טְהוֹרָה הִיא, אַתָּה	shennatatta bi tehora hi, atta
בְרָאתָהּ וְאַתָּה יְצַרְתָּהּ וְאַתָּה	beratah ve'atta yetsartah ve'atta
נְפַחְתָּהּ בִּי וְאַתָּה מְשַׁמְּרָהּ בְּקִרְבִּי,	nefaḥtah bi ve'atta meshammerah beḳirbi,
וּלְכֵן כָּל זְמַן שֶׁהַנְּשָׁמָה	velachen kol zeman shehanneshama
בְּקִרְבִּי מוֹדֶה אֲנִי לְפָנֶיךָ, יְהֹוָה	beḳirbi modé ani lefanecha, Adonai
אֱלֹהַי וֵאלֹהֵי אֲבוֹתַי. בָּרוּךְ אַתָּה	Elohai velohé avotai. Baruch atta
יְהֹוָה שׁוֹמֵר וּפוֹדֶה נַפְשׁוֹת חֲסִידָיו:	Adonai shomer ufodé nafshot ḥasidav:
שְׁמַע יִשְׂרָאֵל, יְהֹוָה אֱלֹהֵינוּ	Shemaʿ Yisra'el, Adonai Elohenu
יְהֹוָה ׀ אֶחָד: אֶחָד אֱלֹהֵינוּ, גָּדוֹל	Adonai Eḥad: ḥad Elohenu, gadol
אֲדֹנֵינוּ, קָדוֹשׁ וְנוֹרָא שְׁמוֹ	Adonenu, ḳadosh venora shemo
לְעוֹלָם וָעֶד:	leʿolam vaʿed:

I GIVE THANKS *before You, living and eternal King, for You have restored within me my soul with compassion; abundant is Your faithfulness! My God, the soul that You gave me is pure; You created it and fashioned it and You blew it into me and You preserve it within me. Therefore, all the time that the soul is within me, I give thanks before You, Adonai, my God and God of my fathers. Blessed are You, Adonai, Who keeps and delivers the souls of His followers.*

HEAR, O ISRAEL: *Adonai is our God; Adonai is one. One is our God, great is our Lord, holy and awesome is His name, forever and ever.*

וְאָהַבְתָּ אֵת יְהוָה אֱלֹהֶיךָ,
בְּכָל־לְבָבְךָ וּבְכָל־נַפְשְׁךָ
וּבְכָל־מְאֹדֶךָ: וְהָיוּ הַדְּבָרִים
הָאֵלֶּה, אֲשֶׁר אָנֹכִי מְצַוְּךָ הַיּוֹם
עַל־לְבָבֶךָ: וְשִׁנַּנְתָּם לְבָנֶיךָ
וְדִבַּרְתָּ בָּם, בְּשִׁבְתְּךָ בְּבֵיתֶךָ
וּבְלֶכְתְּךָ בַדֶּרֶךְ וּבְשָׁכְבְּךָ
וּבְקוּמֶךָ: וּקְשַׁרְתָּם לְאוֹת עַל־יָדֶךָ,
וְהָיוּ לְטֹטָפֹת בֵּין עֵינֶיךָ: וּכְתַבְתָּם
עַל־מְזֻזוֹת בֵּיתֶךָ וּבִשְׁעָרֶיךָ: בָּרוּךְ
יְהוָה לְעוֹלָם, אָמֵן | וְאָמֵן:

Ve'ahavta et Adonai Elohecha,
bechol levavecha uvchol nafshecha
uvchol me'odecha: Vehayu haddevarim
ha'ellé, asher anochi metsavvecha hayyom
ʿal levavecha: Veshinnantam levanecha
vedibbarta bam, beshivtecha bevetecha
uvlechtecha vadderech uvshochbecha
uvḳumecha: Uḳshartam le'ot ʿal yadecha,
vehayu letotafot ben ʿenecha: Uchtavtam
ʿal mezuzot betecha uvishʿarecha: Baruch
Adonai leʿolam, Amen ve'amen:

AND YOU SHALL LOVE *Adonai your God with all your heart, and with all your soul, and with all your might. Take to heart these instructions with which I charge you this day. You shall teach them diligently to your children and shall talk of them when you sit in your house and when you walk by the way and when you lie down and when you rise up. Bind them as a sign on your hand, and they shall be as a remembrance between your eyes. Write them on the door-posts of your house and on your gates. Blessed be Adonai forevermore; Amen, and Amen.*

A PRAYER AFTER WAKING UP

(For Females)

מוֹדָה אֲנִי לְפָנֶיךָ מֶלֶךְ חַי וְקַיָּם	Moda ani lefanecha melech ḥai veḳayyam
שֶׁהֶחֱזַרְתָּ בִּי נִשְׁמָתִי בְּחֶמְלָה,	sheheḥezarta bi nishmati beḥemla,
רַבָּה אֱמוּנָתֶךָ: אֱלֹהַי, נְשָׁמָה	rabba emunatecha: Elohai, neshama
שֶׁנָּתַתָּ בִּי טְהוֹרָה הִיא, אַתָּה	shennatatta bi tehora hi, atta
בְּרָאתָהּ וְאַתָּה יְצַרְתָּהּ וְאַתָּה	beratah ve'atta yetsartah ve'atta
נְפַחְתָּהּ בִּי וְאַתָּה מְשַׁמְּרָהּ בְּקִרְבִּי,	nefaḥtah bi ve'atta meshammerah beḳirbi,
וְלָכֵן כָּל זְמַן שֶׁהַנְּשָׁמָה	velachen kol zeman shehanneshama
בְּקִרְבִּי מוֹדָה אֲנִי לְפָנֶיךָ, יְהֹוָה	beḳirbi moda ani lefanecha, Adonai
אֱלֹהַי וֵאלֹהֵי אֲבוֹתַי. בָּרוּךְ אַתָּה	Elohai velohé avotai. Baruch atta
יְהֹוָה שׁוֹמֵר וּפוֹדֶה נַפְשׁוֹת חֲסִידָיו:	Adonai shomer ufodé nafshot ḥasidav:
שְׁמַע יִשְׂרָאֵל, יְהֹוָה אֱלֹהֵינוּ	Shemaʿ Yisra'el, Adonai Elohenu
יְהֹוָה | אֶחָד: אֶחָד אֱלֹהֵינוּ, גָּדוֹל	Adonai Eḥad: eḥad elohenu, gadol
אֲדֹנֵינוּ, קָדוֹשׁ וְנוֹרָא שְׁמוֹ	Adonenu, ḳadosh venora shemo
לְעוֹלָם וָעֶד:	leʿolam vaʿed:

I GIVE THANKS *before You, living and eternal King, for You have restored within me my soul with compassion; abundant is Your faithfulness! My God, the soul that You gave me is pure; You created it and fashioned it and You blew it into me and You preserve it within me. Therefore, all the time that the soul is within me, I give thanks before You, Adonai, my God and God of my fathers. Blessed are You, Adonai, Who keeps and delivers the souls of His followers.*

HEAR, O ISRAEL: *Adonai is our God; Adonai is one. One is our God, great is our Lord, holy and awesome is His name, forever and ever.*

וְאָהַבְתָּ אֵת יְהוָה אֱלֹהֶיךָ,
בְּכָל־לְבָבְךָ וּבְכָל־נַפְשְׁךָ
וּבְכָל־מְאֹדֶךָ: וְהָיוּ הַדְּבָרִים
הָאֵלֶּה, אֲשֶׁר אָנֹכִי מְצַוְּךָ הַיּוֹם
עַל־לְבָבֶךָ: וְשִׁנַּנְתָּם לְבָנֶיךָ
וְדִבַּרְתָּ בָּם, בְּשִׁבְתְּךָ בְּבֵיתֶךָ
וּבְלֶכְתְּךָ בַדֶּרֶךְ וּבְשָׁכְבְּךָ
וּבְקוּמֶךָ: וּקְשַׁרְתָּם לְאוֹת עַל־יָדֶךָ,
וְהָיוּ לְטֹטָפֹת בֵּין עֵינֶיךָ: וּכְתַבְתָּם
עַל־מְזֻזוֹת בֵּיתֶךָ וּבִשְׁעָרֶיךָ: בָּרוּךְ
יְהוָה לְעוֹלָם, אָמֵן | וְאָמֵן:

Ve'ahavta et Adonai Elohecha,
bechol levavecha uvchol nafshecha
uvchol me'odecha: Vehayu haddevarim
ha'ellé, asher anochi metsavvecha hayyom
'al levavecha: Veshinnantam levanecha
vedibbarta bam, beshivtecha bevetecha
uvlechtecha vadderech uvshochbecha
uvḳumecha: Uḳshartam le'ot 'al yadecha,
vehayu letotafot ben 'enecha: Uchtavtam
'al mezuzot betecha uvish'arecha: Baruch
Adonai le'olam, Amen ve'amen:

AND YOU SHALL LOVE *Adonai your God with all your heart, and with all your soul, and with all your might. Take to heart these instructions with which I charge you this day. You shall teach them diligently to your children and shall talk of them when you sit in your house and when you walk by the way and when you lie down and when you rise up. Bind them as a sign on your hand, and they shall be as a remembrance between your eyes. Write them on the door-posts of your house and on your gates. Blessed be Adonai forevermore; Amen, and Amen.*

A PRAYER BEFORE TRAVELING

יְהִי רָצוֹן מִלְּפָנֶיךָ יְהֹוָה אֱלֹהַי	Yehi ratson millefanecha Adonai Elohai
וֵאלֹהֵי אֲבוֹתַי, שֶׁתּוֹלִיכֵנִי בְּשָׁלוֹם,	velohé avotai, shettolicheni beshalom,
וְתַדְרִיכֵנִי בְּשָׁלוֹם, וְתַגִּיעֵנִי לִמְחוֹז	vetadricheni beshalom, vetaggiʿeni limḥoz
חֶפְצִי בְּשָׁלוֹם, וְתַצְלִיחַ דַּרְכִּי	ḥeftsi beshalom, vetatsliaḥ darki
וּתְשִׁיבֵנִי אֶל בֵּיתִי בְּשָׁלוֹם, וּתְקַיֵּם	utshiveni el beti beshalom, utḳayyem
עָלַי מִקְרָא שֶׁכָּתוּב, וְהִנֵּה אָנֹכִי	ʿalai miḳra shekkatuv: Vehinné anochi
עִמָּךְ וּשְׁמַרְתִּיךָ בְּכֹל אֲשֶׁר־תֵּלֵךְ:	ʿimmach ushmarticha bechol asher telech:
וְתַצִּילֵנִי מֵאוֹיֵב וְאוֹרֵב עַל	Vetats-tsileni meʾoyev veʾorev ʿal
הַדֶּרֶךְ וּמִכָּל פֻּרְעָנֻיּוֹת	hadderech umikkol purʿanuyot badderech,
בַּדֶּרֶךְ, וְתִשְׁמַע כָּל תַּחֲנוּנַי, כִּי	vetishmaʿ kol taḥanunai, ki
אַתָּה שׁוֹמֵעַ תְּפִלַּת כָּל פֶּה. בָּרוּךְ	atta shomeʾaʿ tefillat kol pé. Baruch
יְהֹוָה לְעוֹלָם, אָמֵן׀ וְאָמֵן:	Adonai leʿolam, amen veʾamen:

MAY IT BE THE WILL *before You, Adonai, my God and the God of my fathers, that You will lead me in peace, and You will direct me in peace, and You will make me reach my destination in peace, and You will make my passage successful and return me to my home in peace, and apply to me what is written: "And, behold, I am with you, and I will protect you wherever you go," and You will save me from all the enemies and ambushers on the road, and from all the bad things that may happen on the road, and You will hear all my pleas, because You hear the prayer of everybody. Blessed be Adonai forevermore; Amen, and Amen.*

Blessings for Specific Occasions

ברכות לאירועים מיוחדים

BIRKAT HA-GOMEL

Upon Being Saved from a Life-Threatening Situation, including Illness

בָּרוּךְ אַתָּה יְהוָֹה אֱלֹהֵינוּ מֶלֶךְ	Baruch atta Adonai Elohenu melech
הָעוֹלָם, הַיּוֹדֵעַ צָרַת נַפְשִׁי וּמִכָּל	haʿolam, hayyodeʾaʿ tsarat nafshi umikkol
דָּבָר רָע הוֹשִׁיעַנִי, וּמִצָּרָה הוֹצִיאַנִי	davar raʿ hoshiʿani, umits-tsara hotsiʾani
וּגְאָלַנִי, וְעַל רַגְלַי הֱקִימַנִי, וְאֶל	ugalani, veʿal raglai hekimani veʾel
רְוָחָה הֱבִיאַנִי: בָּרוּךְ אַתָּה יְהוָֹה	revaḥa heviʾani: Baruch atta Adonai
פּוֹדֶה נֶפֶשׁ עֲבָדָיו:	podé nefesh ʿavadav:
★ צוּר שֶׁגְּמָלְךָ טוֹב הוּא יִגְמָלְךָ	★ Tsur sheggemalecha tov hu yigmolcha
טוֹב לָעַד סֶלָה:	tov laʿad sela:

BLESSED *are You, Adonai, our God, King of the universe, Who knows the distress of my soul and Who saved me from all evil things and Who brought my soul out of trouble and delivered me and made me stand on my feet and brought me relief. Blessed are You, Adonai, the redeemer of His worshipers.*

★ *The Rock, Who rewarded you with good, will reward you with good forever. Selah.*

UPON VISITING THE PLACE OF A PERSONAL MIRACLE

בָּרוּךְ אַתָּה יְהוָֹה אֱלֹהֵינוּ מֶלֶךְ	Baruch atta Adonai Elohenu melech
הָעוֹלָם, שֶׁעָשָׂה לִי נֵס בַּמָּקוֹם הַזֶּה:	haʿolam, sheʿasa li nes bammakom hazzé:

BLESSED *are You, Adonai, our God, King of the universe, Who made a miracle for me at this place.*

UPON HEARING GOOD NEWS

בָּרוּךְ אַתָּה יְהוָֹה אֱלֹהֵינוּ מֶלֶךְ	Baruch atta Adonai Elohenu melech
הָעוֹלָם, הַטּוֹב וְהַמֵּיטִיב:	haʿolam, hattov vehammetiv:

BLESSED *are You, Adonai, our God, King of the universe, Who is good and does good.*

UPON HEARING BAD NEWS OR LOSING SOMETHING

בָּרוּךְ אַתָּה יְהֹוָה אֱלֹהֵינוּ מֶלֶךְ	Baruch atta Adonai Elohenu melech
הָעוֹלָם, דַּיַּן הָאֱמֶת:	haʿolam, dayyan haʾemet:

BLESSED are You, Adonai, our God, King of the universe, Who is the True Judge.

UPON FINDING SOMETHING YOU LOST

בָּרוּךְ אַתָּה יְהֹוָה אֱלֹהֵינוּ מֶלֶךְ	Baruch atta Adonai Elohenu melech
הָעוֹלָם, הַמַּחֲזִיר אֲבֵדָה לִבְעָלֶיהָ:	haʿolam, hammaḥazir aveda livʿaleha:

BLESSED are You, Adonai, our God, King of the universe, Who brings lost property to its owner.

UPON NEWNESS

Buying something new, doing something new, eating new fruits of the season

בָּרוּךְ אַתָּה יְהֹוָה אֱלֹהֵינוּ מֶלֶךְ	Baruch atta Adonai Elohenu melech
הָעוֹלָם, שֶׁהֶחֱיָנוּ וְקִיְּמָנוּ	haʿolam, sheheḥeyanu veḳiyyemanu
וְהִגִּיעָנוּ לַזְּמַן הַזֶּה:	vehiggiʿanu lazzeman hazzé:

BLESSED are You, Adonai, our God, King of the universe, Who has kept us alive, sustained us, and enabled us to reach this season.

UPON WEARING TSITSIT

בָּרוּךְ אַתָּה יְהֹוָה אֱלֹהֵינוּ מֶלֶךְ	Baruch atta Adonai Elohenu melech
הָעוֹלָם אֲשֶׁר קִדְּשָׁנוּ בְּמִצְווֹתָיו	haʿolam asher ḳiddeshanu bemitsvotav
וְצִוָּנוּ לִלְבֹּשׁ אַרְבַּע כְּנָפוֹת בְּצִיצִית:	vetsivvanu lilbosh arbaʿ kenafot betsitsit:

BLESSED are You, Adonai, our God, King of the universe, Who has sanctified us with His commandments, and commanded us to wear a four-cornered garment with fringes.

UPON SEEING THE NEW MOON

בָּרוּךְ אַתָּה יְהֹוָה אֱלֹהֵינוּ מֶלֶךְ
הָעוֹלָם, מְחַדֵּשׁ חֳדָשִׁים בְּסִימָן
טוֹב לְעַמּוֹ יִשְׂרָאֵל וּלְכָל הָעוֹלָם:

Baruch atta Adonai Elohenu melech
haʿolam, meḥaddesh ḥodashim besiman
tov leʿammo Yisraʾel ulchol haʿolam:

BLESSED are You, Adonai, our God, King of the universe, Who establishes months with a good sign for His people, Israel, and for the whole world.

UPON THE DEDICATION OF A HOUSE

בָּרוּךְ אַתָּה יְהֹוָה אֱלֹהֵינוּ מֶלֶךְ
הָעוֹלָם, שֶׁהֶחֱיָנוּ וְקִיְּמָנוּ
וְהִגִּיעָנוּ לַזְּמַן הַזֶּה:

Baruch atta Adonai Elohenu melech
haʿolam, sheheḥeyanu veḳiyyemanu
vehiggiʿanu lazzeman hazzé:

אָנָּא אֱלֹהֵינוּ וֵאלֹהֵי אֲבוֹתֵינוּ
בְּרַחֲמֶיךָ הָרַבִּים, הַקֵּם אֶת
הַבַּיִת הַזֶּה לְאֹרֶךְ יָמִים, וְיִהְיֶה
הַבַּיִת הַזֶּה פָּתוּחַ לִרְוָחָה לַעֲנִיִּים
וְאוֹרְחִים כָּל הַיָּמִים, וּבֵית וַעַד
לַחֲכָמִים. וְיִזְכּוּ בְּנֵי הַבַּיִת הַזֶּה
לָדוּר בּוֹ בְּשָׁלוֹם וּבְחַיִּים אֲרֻכִּים,
מְבוֹרָכִים וּנְעִימִים.

Anna Elohenu velohé avotenu
beraḥamecha harabbim, haḳḳem et
habbayit hazzé leʾorech yamim, veyihyé
habbayit hazzé patuaḥ lirvaḥa laʿaniyyim
veʾoreḥim, kol hayyamim, uvet vaʿad
laḥachamim. Veyizku bené habbayit hazzé
ladur bo beshalom uvḥayyim arukkim,
mevorachim unʿimim.

BLESSED are You, Adonai, our God, King of the universe, Who has kept us alive, sustained us, and enabled us to reach this season.

PLEASE, our God and God of our fathers, in Your vast mercy, let this home stand for a long time, and let it be open for poor persons and guests all the days, and a meeting place for scholars. And may the dwellers of this house merit to live in it in peace and have a long, blessed, and pleasant life. And let them sit in it, safely, calmly, peacefully, and pleasantly.

וְיֵשְׁבוּ לָבֶטַח בּוֹ בְּהַשְׁקֵט וּבְשַׁלְוָה	Veyeshevu lavetaḥ bo behashḳet uvshalva
וּבִמְנוּחָה. וְקַיֵּם עַל בְּנֵי הַבַּיִת	uvimnuḥa. Veḳayyem ʿal bené habbayit
הַזֶּה מִקְרָא שֶׁכָּתוּב: "וּבָנוּ בָתִּים	hazzé miḳra shekkatuv: uvanu vattim
וְיָשָׁבוּ, וְנָטְעוּ כְרָמִים וְאָכְלוּ	veyashavu, venateʿu cheramim veʾachelu
פִּרְיָם:"	piryam:
יְבָרֶכְךָ יְהוָה וְיִשְׁמְרֶךָ:	Yevarechecha Adonai veyishmerecha:
יָאֵר יְהוָה ׀ פָּנָיו אֵלֶיךָ וִיחֻנֶּךָּ:	Yaʾer Adonai panav elecha viḥunnekka:
יִשָּׂא יְהוָה ׀ פָּנָיו אֵלֶיךָ	Yissa Adonai panav elecha
וְיָשֵׂם לְךָ שָׁלוֹם:	veyasem lecha shalom:
בָּרוּךְ יְהוָה לְעוֹלָם,	Baruch Adonai leʿolam,
⋆ אָמֵן ׀ וְאָמֵן:	⋆ Amen veʾamen:

And do unto them as it is written: And they shall build houses, and inhabit them; and they shall plant vineyards, and eat their fruit.

May Adonai bless you, and keep you.
May Adonai shine His face toward you, and be gracious unto you.
May Adonai lift His toward you, and give you peace.
Blessed be Adonai forevermore;

⋆ *Amen, and Amen.*

A PRAYER DURING DIFFICULT TIMES

יְהוָֹה אֱלֹהַי וֵאלֹהֵי אֲבוֹתַי, אַתָּה
יָדַעְתָּ אֶת צָרַת נַפְשִׁי וְאֶת כָּל
מַכְאוֹבַי, כִּי אַתָּה בּוֹחֵן כְּלָיוֹת וָלֵב.
וּבְיָדְךָ כֹּחַ לְהוֹשִׁיעֵנִי וְלַעֲזֹר
לִי וּלְחַזֵּק לַכֹּל. שְׁלַח־אוֹרְךָ
וַאֲמִתְּךָ, הֵמָּה יַנְחוּנִי בְּכָל
דְּרָכָי:

Adonai Elohai velohé avotai, atta
yadaʿta et tsarat nafshi veʾet kol
machʾovai, ki atta boḥen kelayot valev.
Uvyadecha koaḥ lehoshiʿeni velaʿazor
li ulḥazzeḳ lakkol. Shelaḥ orecha
vaʾamittecha, hemma yanḥuni bechol
derachai:

אַל תְּבִיאֵנִי לִידֵי נִסָּיוֹן, אֵל עֶלְיוֹן
קֹנֵה שָׁמַיִם וָאָרֶץ, וְאַל אֶכָּשֵׁל
בְּדִבּוּרַי וּבְמַעֲשַׂי כְּנֶגְדְּךָ
וּכְנֶגֶד בְּנֵי אָדָם. וּסְלַח לְכָל
חַטֹּאותַי וּפְשָׁעַי.

Al teviʾeni lidé nissayon, El ʿElyon
ḳoné shamayim vaʾarets, veʾal ekkashel
bedibburai uvmaʿasai keneḡdecha
uchneḡed bené adam. Uslaḥ lechol
ḥattotai ufshaʿai.

חָנֵּנִי וְרַחֲמֵנִי, שָׁמְרָה לִי אֶת
בְּרִיאוּת גּוּפִי וְהַצִּילֵנִי מִכָּל פְּגָעִים
רָעִים וּמִמַּחֲלוֹת וּמִכָּל גְּזֵרוֹת
קָשׁוֹת.

Ḥonneni veraḥameni, shomra li et
beriʾut gufi vehats-tsileni mikkol peḡaʿim
raʿim umimmaḥalot umikkol gezerot
ḳashot.

ADONAI, *my God and God of my fathers, You know full well the distress of my soul and all my pains, because You test the mind and the heart. And You have the power to save me, to help me, and to make everyone strong. O send out Your light and Your truth; let them lead me on all my ways.*

BRING ME NOT *into temptation, God Most High, Possessor of heaven and earth, and let me not fail by saying or doing something against You or against any human being. And forgive all my sins and iniquities.*

BE GRACIOUS TO ME AND HAVE MERCY ON ME. *Preserve my health and save me from all the bad injuries and diseases and from any bad decrees.*

תֵּן לִי מְנוּחַת נֶפֶשׁ וְרוּחַ, וְהַרְחֵק
מִלִּבִּי כָּל יָגוֹן, אֲנָחָה וְיֵאוּשׁ
וְתֵן לִי כֹּחַ וְעָצְמָה לְקַיֵּם אֶת כָּל
מִצְוֹתֶיךָ. וְזַכֵּנִי לַעֲשׂוֹת צְדָקוֹת
בְּיִשְׂרָאֵל וּבָאָדָם, וְיִשְׂמְחוּ בִּי כָּל
יְרֵאֶיךָ וְגַם אֲנִי אֶשְׂמַח בָּהֶם.

Ten li menuḥat nefesh veruaḥ, veharḥeḳ
millibbi kol yağon, anaḥa veye'ush
veten li koaḥ ve'otsma leḳayyem et kol
mitsvotecha. Vezakkeni la'asot tsedaḳot
beYisra'el uva'adam, veyismeḥu bi kol
yere'echa veğam ani esmaḥ bahem.

שְׁלַח בִּרְכָתְךָ עָלַי וְעַל בֵּיתִי וְעַל
כָּל חֲסִידֶיךָ. הַשְׁבֵּת מִלְחָמוֹת
בֵּין הָעַמִּים וּבַטֵּל שִׂנְאָה בֵּין
בְּנֵי הָאָדָם וּמַלֵּא מִשְׁאֲלוֹת לִבִּי
לְטוֹבָה. וְיִהְיוּ לְרָצוֹן ׀ אִמְרֵי־פִי
וְהֶגְיוֹן לִבִּי לְפָנֶיךָ, יְהוָה צוּרִי
וְגֹאֲלִי: בָּרוּךְ יְהוָה לְעוֹלָם,
אָמֵן ׀ וְאָמֵן:

Shelaḥ birchatecha 'alai ve'al beti ve'al
kol ḥasidecha. Hashbet milḥamot
ben ha'ammim uvattel sina ben
bené ha'adam umallé mishalot libbi
letova. Veyihyu leratson imré fi
veheğyon libbi lefanecha, Adonai tsuri
veğo'ali: Baruch Adonai le'olam
Amen ve'amen:

GRANT my spirit and soul rest, and distance me from any sorrow, groan, and desperation. Give me power and strength to fulfill all Your commandments. Give me the merit to perform charity among Israel and all people. And may all who fear You be pleased with me, and may I be pleased with them.

SEND Your blessings upon me and my home and upon all Your adherents. Put an end to war between the nations and stop hatred between human beings and fulfill my wishes for good. And may the words of my mouth and prayers of my heart be acceptable to You, O Adonai, my Rock and my Redeemer. Blessed be Adonai forevermore; Amen, and Amen.

A PRAYER BEFORE TAKING A TEST

יְהֹוָה אֱלֹהַי וֵאלֹהֵי אֲבוֹתַי, אַתָּה
יָדַעְתָּ אֶת מִשְׁאֲלוֹת לִבִּי, כִּי
אַתָּה בּוֹחֵן כְּלָיוֹת וָלֵב. וּבְיָדְךָ כֹּחַ
לְהוֹשִׁיעֵנִי וְלַעֲזֹר לִי וּלְחַזֵּק לַכֹּל.
שְׁלַח־אוֹרְךָ וַאֲמִתְּךָ הֵמָּה
יַנְחוּנִי בְּכָל דְּרָכָי:

Adonai Elohai velohé avotai, atta
yadaʿta et mishalot libbi, ki
atta boḥen kelayot valev. Uvyadecha koʾaḥ
lehoshiʿeni velaʿazor li ulḥazzeḳ lakkol.
Shelaḥ orecha vaʾamittecha hemma
yanḥuni bechol derachai:

אָנָּא אֱלֹהַי, תֵּן לִי לְשׁוֹן לִמּוּדִים
וַעֲזֹר לִי לְהִתְרַכֵּז וּלְהַצְלִיחַ לִלְמֹד
וְלִזְכֹּר אֶת כָּל הַחֹמֶר לַמִּבְחָן.
עֲזֹר לִי לְהָשִׁיב בַּזְּמַן אֶת
הַתְּשׁוּבוֹת הַנְּכוֹנוֹת שֶׁיִּמְצְאוּ
חֵן בְּעֵינֵי בּוֹחֲנַי וְשֶׁלֹּא יִקְרֶה לִי
שׁוּם בִּלְבּוּל אוֹ הִסּוּס בְּשָׁעַת
הַמִּבְחָן.

Anna Elohai, ten li leshon limmudim
vaʿazor li lehitrakkez ulhatsliaḥ lilmod
velizkor et kol haḥomer lammivḥan.
ʿAzor li lehashiv bazzeman et
hatteshuvot hannechonot sheyyimtseʾu
ḥen beʿené boḥanai veshello yiḳré li
shum bilbul o hissus beshaʿat
hammivḥan.

אָנָּא אֱלֹהַי זַכֵּנִי לְהִתְקַדֵּם
בַּחַיִּים, לְהַצְלִיחַ, לְיַשֵּׂם לְטוֹבָה
אֶת מַה שֶּׁאֲנִי לוֹמֵד וְלַעֲזֹר לִבְנֵי
אָדָם.

Anna Elohai zakkeni lehitḳaddem
baḥayyim, lehatsliaḥ, leyassem letova
et ma sheʾani lomed velaʿazor livné
adam.

ADONAI, my God and God of my fathers, You know my soul's requests, because You test the mind and the heart. And You have the power to help me and to make everyone strong. O send out Your light and Your truth; let them lead me on all my ways.

PLEASE, my God, give me the tongue of learning and help me concentrate and be able to learn and remember all the material for the test. Help me answer all the right answers that

my examiners would like within the allotted time period, and help me so that I will not get confused and I will not hesitate during the test.

PLEASE, my God, help me get ahead in life, and to succeed; and enable me to apply what I learn for good and to help human beings

אָנָּא יְהֹוָה הוֹשִׁיעָה נָּא, אָנָּא	Anna Adonai hoshiʿa na, anna
יְהֹוָה הַצְלִיחָה נָּא: וְיִהְיוּ לְרָצוֹן ׀	Adonai hatsliḥa na: Veyihyu leratson
אִמְרֵי־פִי וְהֶגְיוֹן לִבִּי לְפָנֶיךָ, יְהֹוָה	imré fi vehegyon libbi lefanecha, Adonai
צוּרִי וְגֹאֲלִי: בָּרוּךְ יְהֹוָה לְעוֹלָם,	tsuri vegoʾali: Baruch Adonai leʿolam
אָמֵן ׀ וְאָמֵן:	Amen veʾamen:

O ADONAI, DELIVER US! O Adonai, let us prosper! And may the words of my mouth and prayers of my heart be acceptable to You, O Adonai, my Rock and my Redeemer. Blessed be Adonai forevermore; Amen, and Amen.

A PRAYER FOR HAVING WORTHY FRIENDS

יְהֹוָה אֱלֹהַי וֵאלֹהֵי אֲבוֹתַי, אַתָּה	Adonai Elohai velohé avotai, atta
יָדַעְתָּ אֶת מִשְׁאֲלוֹת לִבִּי, כִּי	yadaʿta et mishʾalot libbi, ki
אַתָּה בּוֹחֵן כְּלָיוֹת וָלֵב. וּבְיָדְךָ כֹּחַ	atta boḥen kelayot valev. Uvyadecha koaḥ
לְהוֹשִׁיעֵנִי וְלַעֲזֹר לִי וּלְחַזֵּק לַכֹּל.	lehoshiʿeni velaʿazor li ulḥazzek lakkol.
שְׁלַח־אוֹרְךָ וַאֲמִתְּךָ הֵמָּה	Shelaḥ orecha vaʾamittecha hemma
יַנְחוּנִי בְּכָל דְּרָכָי:	yanḥuni bechol derachai:
אֱלֹהַי, אַתָּה אָמַרְתָּ כִּי ״לֹא־טוֹב	Elohai, atta amarta ki lo tov
הֱיוֹת הָאָדָם לְבַדּוֹ״ וְכָתוּב: ״טוֹבִים	heyot haʾadam levaddo vechatuv: Tovim
הַשְּׁנַיִם מִן־הָאֶחָד״ וְכֵן:	hash-shenayim min haʾeḥad vechen:
״הִנֵּה מַה־טּוֹב וּמַה־נָּעִים	Hinné ma tov uma naʿim
שֶׁבֶת אַחִים גַּם־יָחַד״.	shevet aḥim gam yaḥad.

MY GOD and God of my fathers, You know full well the distress of my soul, because You test

the mind and the heart. And you have the power to help me and to make everyone strong. O send out Your light and Your truth; let them lead me on all my ways.

MY GOD, *You said, "It is not good for a man to be alone," and it is written: "Two are better than one" and "Behold, how good and how pleasant it is for brethren to dwell together in unity!"*

אָנָּא אָבִי שֶׁבַּשָּׁמַיִם, בַּטֵּל מֵעָלַי	Anna avi shebbashamayim, battel meʿalai
כָּל יֵאוּשׁ וְדִכְדּוּךְ, מַלֵּא לְבָבִי	kol yeʾush vedichduch, mallé levavi
שִׂמְחָה, בִּטָּחוֹן וְאֹשֶׁר. הָכֵן לְבָבִי	simḥa, bittaḥon veʾosher. Hachen levavi
לִרְאוֹת אֶת הַטּוֹב שֶׁבִּבְנֵי הָאָדָם	lirot et hattov shebbivné haʾadam
וַעֲזֹר לָהֶם לִרְאוֹת אֶת הַטּוֹב	vaʿazor lahem lirʾot et hattov
וְהַמַּעֲלוֹת שֶׁבִּי. וְהַטֵּה אֶת לְבַב	vehammaʿalot shebbi. Vehatté et levav
בְּנֵי הָאָדָם אֵלַי לְטוֹבָה וַעֲזֹר לִי	bené haʾadam elai letova vaʿazor li
לִמְצֹא חַבְרֵי אֱמֶת הֲגוּנִים וִישָׁרִים	limtso ḥavré emet hag̱unim visharim
שֶׁיּוֹלִיכוּנִי לְטוֹבָה.	sheyyolichuni letova.
עֲזֹר לָנוּ שֶׁלֹּא תִּהְיֶה כָּל שִׂנְאָה	ʿAzor lanu shello tihyé kol sina
בְּלִבֵּנוּ וְשֶׁנִּמְצָא הַרְבֵּה רַחֲמִים	belibbenu veshennimtsa harbé raḥamim
וְאַהֲבָה. וְיִהְיוּ לְרָצוֹן ׀ אִמְרֵי־פִי	veʾahava. Veyihyu leratson imré fi
וְהֶגְיוֹן לִבִּי לְפָנֶיךָ, יְהוָה צוּרִי	veheg̱yon libbi lefanecha, Adonai tsuri
וְגֹאֲלִי: בָּרוּךְ יְהוָה לְעוֹלָם,	veg̱oʾali: Baruch Adonai leʿolam
אָמֵן ׀ וְאָמֵן:	Amen veʾamen:

PLEASE, *my Father in heaven, remove from me any desperation and sadness; fill my soul with happiness, confidence, and joy. Prepare my heart to see the good sides of all human beings and help them to see my good sides and my good qualities. Steer the hearts of people to me for good, and help me find true, honest, and upright friends who will guide me to good ways.*

HELP *us all to not have hate in our hearts and to find much mercy and love. And may the words of my mouth and prayers of my heart be acceptable to You, O Adonai, my Rock and my Redeemer. Blessed be Adonai forevermore; Amen, and Amen.*

A BLESSING TO HEAL THE SICK

יְהֹוָה אֱלֹהֵי יִשְׂרָאֵל בְּרַחֲמָיו
הָרַבִּים וּבַחֲסָדָיו הַגְּדוֹלִים
וְהַנֶּאֱמָנִים, הוּא יָחֹן וִירַחֵם
וְיַחְמֹל עַל מַעֲלַת ______ וְכָל
חוֹלֵי עַמּוֹ בֵּית יִשְׂרָאֵל שֶׁנָּפְלוּ
בְּחֹלִי. אֱלֹהֵי יִשְׂרָאֵל בְּרַחֲמָיו
הָרַבִּים יְחַיֵּהֶם מֵחָלְיָם
וְיִרְפָּאֵם מִמַּכְאוֹבָם, וִירַחֵם
עֲלֵיהֶם: וִיקִימֵם וְיַחֲלִימֵם
מִמַּחֲלָתָם: וִיקַיֵּם עֲלֵיהֶם מִקְרָא
שֶׁכָּתוּב: וַיֹּאמֶר אִם־שָׁמוֹעַ תִּשְׁמַע
לְקוֹל ׀ יְהֹוָה אֱלֹהֶיךָ וְהַיָּשָׁר
בְּעֵינָיו תַּעֲשֶׂה וְהַאֲזַנְתָּ לְמִצְוֺתָיו
וְשָׁמַרְתָּ כָּל־חֻקָּיו, כָּל־הַמַּחֲלָה
אֲשֶׁר־שַׂמְתִּי בְמִצְרַיִם לֹא־אָשִׂים
עָלֶיךָ כִּי אֲנִי יְהֹוָה רֹפְאֶךָ:

Adonai Elohé Yisra'el beraḥamav
harabbim uvaḥasadav haggedolim
vehanne'emanim, hu yaḥon viraḥem
veyaḥmol ʿal maʿalat ______ vechol
ḥolé ʿammo bet Yisra'el shennafelu
beḥoli. Elohé Yisra'el beraḥamav
harabbim yeḥayyehem meḥolyam
veyiirpa'em mimmach'ovam viraḥem
ʿalehem: Viḳimem veyaḥalimem
mimmaḥalatam: Viḳayyem ʿalehem miḳra
shekkatuv: Vayyomer im shamoaʿ tishmaʿ
leḳol Adonai Elohecha vehayyashar
beʿenav taʿasé veha'azanta lemitsvotav
veshamarta kol ḥuḳḳav, kol hammaḥala
asher samti vemitsrayim lo asim
ʿalecha ki ani Adonai rofe'echa:

MAY ADONAI, *God of Israel, in His great mercy and great kindness, show favor and have mercy and have sorrow upon the honorable ______ and all the suffering ones of His people, the House of Israel, who have fallen ill. May the God of Israel, in His great mercy, revive them from their illness, and heal them from their suffering, and show mercy to them, and raise them again, and let them recuperate from their sickness. And do unto them as it is written: And He said, if you will diligently listen to the voice of Adonai, your God, and will do that which is right in His sight, and will heed His commandments, and keep all His statutes, I will put none of these diseases upon you, which I have brought upon the Egyptians; for I am Adonai that heals you.*

וְהֵסִיר יְהֹוָה מִמְּךָ כָּל־חֹלִי,
וְכָל־מַדְוֵי מִצְרַיִם הָרָעִים אֲשֶׁר
יָדַעְתָּ לֹא יְשִׂימָם בָּךְ וּנְתָנָם
בְּכָל־שֹׂנְאֶיךָ: רְפָאֵם יְהֹוָה
וְיֵרָפְאוּ הוֹשִׁיעֵם וְיִוָּשֵׁעוּ כִּי
תְהִלָּתִי אָתָּה: אֵל נָא, רְפָא נָא
לָהֶם: אֵל נָא, רְפָא נָא לָהֶם: אֵל
נָא, רְפָא נָא לָהֶם: יְהֹוָה הוֹשִׁיעָה
הַמֶּלֶךְ יַעֲנֵנוּ בְיוֹם־קָרְאֵנוּ:
בָּרוּךְ יְהֹוָה לְעוֹלָם,
⋆ אָמֵן ׀ וְאָמֵן:

Vehesir Adonai mimmecha kol ḥoli,
vechol madvé mitsrayim hara‘im asher
yada‘ta lo yesimam bach untanam
bechol sone’echa: Refa’em Adonai
veyerafe’u hoshi‘em veyivvashe‘u ki
tehillati atta: El na, refa na
lahem: El na, refa na lahem: El
na, refa na lahem: Adonai hoshi‘a
hammelech ya‘anenu veyom ḳorenu:
Baruch Adonai le‘olam,
⋆ Amen ve’amen:

AND ADONAI WILL TAKE ALL sickness from you, and will put none of the evil diseases of Egypt, which you know, upon you; but will lay them upon all those who hate you. Heal them, Adonai, and they shall be healed; save them, and they shall be saved; for You are my praise. Heal them now, O God, I beseech You. Heal them now, O God, I beseech You. Heal them now, O God, I beseech You. Save, Adonai; the King will answer us on the day when we call. Blessed be Adonai forevermore;

⋆Amen, and Amen.

A BLESSING IN MEMORY OF THE DEPARTED

(For a Male)

זִכְרוֹן טוֹב וְחֵן וָחֶסֶד וְרַחֲמִים	Zichron tov veḥen vaḥesed veraḥamim
וְחֶמְלָה וַחֲנִינָה וְרָצוֹן וְכַפָּרָה	veḥemla vaḥanina veratson vechappara
מִלִּפְנֵי אֵל אֱלֹהֵי הָרוּחוֹת לְכָל	millifné El Elohé haruḥot lechol
בָּשָׂר שֶׁהוּא צוּר עוֹלָמִים, עַל־נֶפֶשׁ	basar shehu tsur ʿolamim, ʿal nefesh
כְּבוֹד מַעֲלַת _______, שֶׁעָבַר	kevod maʿalat _______ , sheʿavar
מִן הָעוֹלָם הַזֶּה בְּמַאֲמַר אֱלֹהֵי	min haʿolam hazzé bemaʾamar Elohé
יִשְׂרָאֵל, בְּחֶפְצוֹ וּבִרְצוֹנוֹ, וְהָלַךְ	Yisraʾel, beḥeftso uvirtsono, vehalach
לְבֵית־עוֹלָמוֹ בְּשֵׁם טוֹב וְזֵכֶר טוֹב	levet ʿolamo beshem tov vezecher tov
וּבְמַעֲשִׂים טוֹבִים. אֱלֹהֵי יִשְׂרָאֵל	uvmaʿasim tovim. Elohé Yisraʾel
יִזְכְּרֵהוּ בִּרְצוֹן עַמּוֹ,	yizkerehu birtson ʿammo,
★ אָמֵן,	★ Amen,
וְיִפְקְדֵהוּ בִּישׁוּעָתוֹ,	veyifkedehu bishuʿato,
★ אָמֵן,	★ Amen,

MAY THERE BE A GOOD REMEMBRANCE, and grace, and favor, and mercy, and compassion, and amnesty, and willingness, and atonement from God, the God of the spirits of all flesh, Who is the everlasting rock, upon the soul of the honorable _______ who has passed away from this world by the order of the God of Israel in His will and His wish, and passed on to his eternal home with a good name and a good memory and good deeds. May the God of Israel remember him when He shows favor to His people,

★ *Amen*

And visit him with His salvation,

★ *Amen*

כַּכָּתוּב: ״זָכְרֵנִי יְהוָה בִּרְצוֹן
עַמֶּךָ, פָּקְדֵנִי בִּישׁוּעָתֶךָ: לִרְאוֹת ׀
בְּטוֹבַת בְּחִירֶיךָ לִשְׂמֹחַ בְּשִׂמְחַת
גּוֹיֶךָ לְהִתְהַלֵּל עִם־נַחֲלָתֶךָ:״
וְיִתֵּן חֶלְקוֹ וְגוֹרָלוֹ עִם
הַצַּדִּיקִים וְעִם הַמַּשְׂכִּילִים,
כַּכָּתוּב: ״וְהַמַּשְׂכִּלִים יַזְהִרוּ
כְּזֹהַר הָרָקִיעַ, וּמַצְדִּיקֵי הָרַבִּים
כַּכּוֹכָבִים לְעוֹלָם וָעֶד:״ נַפְשׁוֹ
בְּטוֹב תָּלִין וְזַרְעוֹ וּמִשְׁפַּחְתּוֹ יִירְשׁוּ
אָרֶץ, יָבוֹא שָׁלוֹם יָנוּחַ עַל מִשְׁכָּבוֹ,
הֹלֵךְ נְכֹחוֹ: וִיקַיֵּם עָלָיו מִקְרָא
שֶׁכָּתוּב: ״יַעְלְזוּ חֲסִידִים בְּכָבוֹד,
יְרַנְּנוּ עַל־מִשְׁכְּבוֹתָם:״, ״אוֹר זָרֻעַ
לַצַּדִּיק, וּלְיִשְׁרֵי־לֵב שִׂמְחָה:

Kakkatuv: Zochreni Adonai birtson
ʿammecha, poḳdeni bishuʿatecha: Lirʾot
betovat beḥirecha lismoaḥ besimḥat
goyecha lehit-hallel ʿim naḥalatecha:
Veyitten ḥelḳo veḡoralo ʿim
hats-tsaddiḳim veʿim hammaskilim,
kakkatuv: Vehammaskilim yazhiru
kezohar haraḳiaʿ, umatsdiḳé harabbim
kakkochavim leʿolam vaʿed: Nafsho
betov talin vezarʿo umishpaḥto yireshu
arets, yavo shalom yanuaḥ ʿal mishkavo,
holech nechoḥo: Viḳayyem ʿalav miḳra
shekkatuv: Yaʿlezu ḥasidim bechavod,
yerannenu ʿal mishkevotam: Or zaruaʿ
lats-tsaddiḳ, ulyishré lev simḥa:

AS IT IS WRITTEN: *Remember me, Adonai, when You show favor to Your people; O visit me with Your salvation that I may see the good of Your chosen ones, that I may rejoice in the gladness of Your nation, that I may glory with Your inheritance. And may He give him his share and lot with the righteous and enlightened ones, as it is written: And the enlightened shall shine like the brightness of the firmament; and those who turn many to righteousness like the stars, forever and ever. May his soul have a good rest and his seed and family inherit the earth: peace enters; he rests in his bed, who walks facing Him. And do unto him as it is written: let the pious be joyful in glory; let them sing aloud upon their beds; light is sown for the righteous, and gladness for the upright of heart.*

שִׂמְחוּ צַדִּיקִים בַּיהֹוָה, וְהוֹדוּ
לְזֵכֶר קָדְשׁוֹ:", "אָז יִבָּקַע כַּשַּׁחַר
אוֹרֶךָ וַאֲרֻכָתְךָ מְהֵרָה תִצְמָח,
וְהָלַךְ לְפָנֶיךָ צִדְקֶךָ, כְּבוֹד
יְהֹוָה יַאַסְפֶךָ:"
* וּמְנוּחָתוֹ בְּגַן־עֵדֶן. אָמֵן.

Simḥu tsaddiḳim badonai, vehodu
lezecher ḳodsho: Az yibbaḳaʿ kash-shaḥar
orecha vaʾaruchatecha mehera titsmaḥ,
vehalach lefanecha tsidḳecha, kevod
Adonai yaʾasfecha:
* Umnuḥato beGan ʿEden. Amen.

REJOICE in Adonai, you righteous; and give thanks to His holy name. Then shall your light break forth like the morning, and your health shall spring forth speedily; and your righteousness shall go before you; the glory of Adonai will gather you in.
* *May he rest in the Garden of Eden, Amen.*

A BLESSING IN MEMORY OF THE DEPARTED

(*For a Female*)

זִכְרוֹן טוֹב וְחֵן וָחֶסֶד וְרַחֲמִים
וְחֶמְלָה וַחֲנִינָה וְרָצוֹן וְכַפָּרָה
מִלִּפְנֵי אֵל אֱלֹהֵי הָרוּחוֹת לְכָל
בָּשָׂר שֶׁהוּא צוּר עוֹלָמִים, עַל־נֶפֶשׁ
כְּבוֹד מַעֲלַת ________, שֶׁעָבְרָה
מִן הָעוֹלָם הַזֶּה בְּמַאֲמַר אֱלֹהֵי
יִשְׂרָאֵל, בְּחֶפְצוֹ וּבִרְצוֹנוֹ, וְהָלְכָה
לְבֵית־עוֹלָמָהּ בְּשֵׁם טוֹב וְזֵכֶר טוֹב
וּבְמַעֲשִׂים טוֹבִים.

Zichron tov veḥen vaḥesed veraḥamim
veḥemla vaḥanina veratson vechappara
millifné El Elohé haruḥot lechol
basar shehu tsur ʿolamim, ʿal nefesh
kevod maʿalat ________, sheʿavera
min haʿolam hazzé bemaʾamar Elohé
Yisraʾel, beḥeftso uvirtsono, vehalecha
levet ʿolamah beshem tov vezecher tov
uvmaʿasim tovim.

MAY THERE BE A GOOD REMEMBRANCE, and grace, and favor, and mercy, and compassion, and amnesty, and willingness, and atonement from God, the God of the spirits of all flesh, Who is the everlasting rock, upon the soul of the honorable ________ who has passed away from this world by the order of the God of Israel in His will and His wish, and passed on to her eternal home with good name and a good memory and good deeds.

אֱלֹהֵי יִשְׂרָאֵל יִזְכְּרֶהָ בִּרְצוֹן עַמּוֹ,	Elohé Yisra'el yizkereha birtson ʿammo,
* אָמֵן,	* Amen,
וְיִפְקְדֶהָ בִּישׁוּעָתוֹ,	veyifḳedeha bishuʿato,
* אָמֵן,	* Amen,
כַּכָּתוּב: "זָכְרֵנִי יְהוָה בִּרְצוֹן	Kakkatuv: Zochreni Adonai birtson
עַמֶּךָ, פָּקְדֵנִי בִּישׁוּעָתֶךָ: לִרְאוֹת	ʿammecha, poḳdeni bishuʿatecha: Lirot
בְּטוֹבַת בְּחִירֶיךָ לִשְׂמֹחַ בְּשִׂמְחַת	betovat beḥirecha lismoaḥ besimḥat
גּוֹיֶךָ, לְהִתְהַלֵּל עִם־נַחֲלָתֶךָ:"	goyecha lehit-hallel ʿim naḥalatecha:
וְיִתֵּן חֶלְקָהּ וְגוֹרָלָהּ עִם	Veyitten ḥelḳah veḡoralah ʿim
הַצַּדִּיקִים וְעִם הַמַּשְׂכִּילִים,	hats-tsaddiḳim veʿim hammaskilim,
כַּכָּתוּב: "וְהַמַּשְׂכִּלִים יַזְהִרוּ	kakkatuv: Vehammaskilim yazhiru
כְּזֹהַר הָרָקִיעַ, וּמַצְדִּיקֵי הָרַבִּים	kezohar haraḳiaʿ, umatsdiḳé harabbim
כַּכּוֹכָבִים לְעוֹלָם וָעֶד:" נַפְשָׁהּ	kakkochavim leʿolam vaʿed: Nafshah
בְּטוֹב תָּלִין וְזַרְעָהּ וּמִשְׁפַּחְתָּהּ	betov talin vezarʿah umishpaḥtah
יִירְשׁוּ אָרֶץ, יָבוֹא שָׁלוֹם תָּנוּחַ עַל	yireshu arets, yavo shalom yanuaḥ ʿal
מִשְׁכָּבָהּ, הֹלֵךְ נְכֹחוֹ:	mishkavah, holech nechoḥo:

May the God of Israel remember her when He shows favor to His people,
* *Amen*

And visit her with His salvation,
* *Amen*

AS IT IS WRITTEN: *Remember me, Adonai, when You show favor to Your people; O visit me with Your salvation that I may see the good of Your chosen ones, that I may rejoice in the gladness of Your nation, that I may glory with Your inheritance. And may He give her her share and lot with the righteous and enlightened ones, as it is written: And the enlightened shall shine like the brightness of the firmament; and those who turn many to righteousness like the stars forever and ever. May her soul have a good rest and her seed and family will inherit the earth: peace enters; she rests in her bed, who walks facing Him.*

וִיקַיֵּם עָלֶיהָ מִקְרָא שֶׁכָּתוּב:
”יַעְלְזוּ חֲסִידִים בְּכָבוֹד, יְרַנְּנוּ
עַל־מִשְׁכְּבוֹתָם:”, ”אוֹר זָרֻעַ
לַצַּדִּיק, וּלְיִשְׁרֵי־לֵב שִׂמְחָה:
שִׂמְחוּ צַדִּיקִים בַּיהוָה וְהוֹדוּ
לְזֵכֶר קָדְשׁוֹ:”, ”אָז יִבָּקַע כַּשַּׁחַר
אוֹרֶךָ וַאֲרֻכָתְךָ מְהֵרָה תִצְמָח
וְהָלַךְ לְפָנֶיךָ צִדְקֶךָ, כְּבוֹד
יְהוָה יַאַסְפֶךָ:”
* וּמְנוּחָתָהּ בְּגַן־עֵדֶן. אָמֵן.

Viḳayyem ʿaleha miḳra shekkatuv:
Yaʿlezu ḥasidim bechavod, yerannenu
ʿal mishkevotam: Or zaruaʿ
lats-tsaddiḳ, ulyishré lev simḥa:
Simḥu tsaddiḳim badonai, vehodu
lezecher ḳodsho: Az yibbaḳaʿ kash-shaḥar
orecha va'aruchatecha mehera titsmaḥ,
vehalach lefanecha tsidḳecha, kevod
Adonai ya'asfecha:
* Umnuḥatah beḠan ʿEden. Amen.

And do unto her as it is written: Let the pious be joyful in glory; let them sing aloud upon their beds; light is sown for the righteous, and gladness for the upright of heart. Rejoice in Adonai, you righteous; and give thanks to His holy name. Then shall your light break forth like the morning, and your health shall spring forth speedily; and your righteousness shall go before you; the glory of Adonai will gather you in.

* *May she rest in the Garden of Eden, Amen.*

A BLESSING IN MEMORY OF THE DEPARTED

(For Many Individuals)

זִכְרוֹן טוֹב וְחֵן וָחֶסֶד וְרַחֲמִים	Zichron tov veḥen vaḥesed veraḥamim
וְחֶמְלָה וַחֲנִינָה וְרָצוֹן וְכַפָּרָה	veḥemla vaḥanina veratson vechappara
מִלִּפְנֵי אֵל אֱלֹהֵי הָרוּחוֹת לְכָל	millifné El Elohé haruḥot lechol
בָּשָׂר שֶׁהוּא צוּר עוֹלָמִים,	basar shehu tsur ʿolamim,
עַל־נֶפֶשׁ כְּבוֹד מַעֲלַת ________	ʿal nefesh kevod maʿalat ________ ,
וְכָל מֵתֵי עַמּוֹ בֵּית יִשְׂרָאֵל, שֶׁעָבְרוּ	vechol meté ʿammo bet Yisraʾel, sheʿaveru
מִן הָעוֹלָם הַזֶּה בְּמַאֲמַר אֱלֹהֵי	min haʿolam hazzé bemaʾamar Elohé
יִשְׂרָאֵל, בְּחֶפְצוֹ וּבִרְצוֹנוֹ, וְהָלְכוּ	Yisraʾel, beḥeftso uvirtsono, vehalechu
לְבֵית־עוֹלָמָם בְּשֵׁם טוֹב וְזֵכֶר טוֹב	levet ʿolamam beshem tov vezecher tov
וּבְמַעֲשִׂים טוֹבִים. אֱלֹהֵי יִשְׂרָאֵל	uvmaʿasim tovim. Elohé Yisraʾel
יִזְכְּרֵם בִּרְצוֹן עַמּוֹ,	yizkerem birtson ʿammo,
★ אָמֵן,	★ Amen,
וְיִפְקְדֵם בִּישׁוּעָתוֹ,	veyifḳedem bishuʿato,
★ אָמֵן,	★ Amen,

MAY THERE BE A GOOD REMEMBRANCE, and grace, and favor, and mercy, and compassion, and willingness, and amnesty from God, the God of the spirits of all flesh, Who is the everlasting rock, upon the soul of the honorable ________ and all the deceased persons of His people, Israel, who have passed away from this world by the order of the God of Israel in His will and His wish, and passed on to their eternal home in good name and good memory and good deeds. May the God of Israel remember them when He shows favor to His people,

★ *Amen*

And visit them with His salvation,

★ *Amen*

כַּכָּתוּב: "זָכְרֵנִי יְהֹוָה בִּרְצוֹן
עַמֶּךָ, פָּקְדֵנִי בִּישׁוּעָתֶךָ: לִרְאוֹת
בְּטוֹבַת בְּחִירֶיךָ לִשְׂמֹחַ בְּשִׂמְחַת
גּוֹיֶךָ, לְהִתְהַלֵּל עִם-נַחֲלָתֶךָ:"
וְיִתֵּן חֶלְקָם וְגוֹרָלָם עִם
הַצַּדִּיקִים וְעִם הַמַּשְׂכִּילִים,
כַּכָּתוּב: "וְהַמַּשְׂכִּלִים יַזְהִרוּ
כְּזֹהַר הָרָקִיעַ וּמַצְדִּיקֵי הָרַבִּים
כַּכּוֹכָבִים לְעוֹלָם וָעֶד:" נַפְשָׁם
בְּטוֹב תָּלִין וְזַרְעָם וּמִשְׁפְּחוֹתֵיהֶם
יִירְשׁוּ אָרֶץ, יָבוֹא שָׁלוֹם יָנוּחוּ עַל-
מִשְׁכְּבוֹתָם, הֹלֵךְ נְכֹחוֹ: וִיקַיֵּם
עֲלֵיהֶם מִקְרָא שֶׁכָּתוּב: "יַעְלְזוּ
חֲסִידִים בְּכָבוֹד, יְרַנְּנוּ עַל-
מִשְׁכְּבוֹתָם:", "אוֹר זָרֻעַ לַצַּדִּיק,
וּלְיִשְׁרֵי-לֵב שִׂמְחָה: שִׂמְחוּ
צַדִּיקִים בַּיהֹוָה, וְהוֹדוּ לְזֵכֶר
קָדְשׁוֹ:"

Kakkatuv: Zochreni Adonai birtson ʿammecha, poḳdeni bishuʿatecha: Lirot betovat beḥirecha lismoaḥ besimḥat goyecha lehit-hallel ʿim naḥalatecha: Veyitten ḥelḳam veḡoralam ʿim hats-tsaddiḳim veʿim hammaskilim, kakkatuv: Vehammaskilim yazhiru kezohar haraḳiaʿ, umatsdiḳé harabbim kakkochavim leʿolam vaʿed: Nafsham betov talin vezarʿam umishpeḥotehem yireshu arets, yavo shalom yanuḥu ʿal mishkevotam, holech nechoḥo: Viḳayyem ʿalehem miḳra shekkatuv: Yaʿlezu ḥasidim bechavod, yerannenu ʿal mishkevotam: Or zaruaʿ lats-tsaddiḳ, ulyishré lev simḥa: Simḥu tsaddiḳim badonai, vehodu lezecher ḳodsho:

AS IT IS WRITTEN: *Remember me, Adonai, when You show favor to Your people; O visit me with Your salvation that I may see the good of Your chosen ones, that I may rejoice in the gladness of Your nation, that I may glory with Your inheritance. And may He give them their share and lot with the righteous and enlightened ones, as it is written: And the enlightened shall shine like the brightness of the firmament; and those who turn many to righteousness like the stars, forever and ever. May their souls have a good rest and their seed and family will inherit the earth: peace enters; they rest in their bed, who walks facing Him. And do unto them as it is written: Let the pious be joyful in glory; let them sing aloud upon their beds; light is sown for the righteous, and gladness for the upright of heart. Rejoice in Adonai, you righteous; and give thanks to His holy name.*

"אָ֣ז יִבָּקַ֤ע כַּשַּׁ֙חַר֙ אוֹרֶ֔ךָ
וַאֲרֻכָתְךָ֖ מְהֵרָ֣ה תִצְמָ֑ח, וְהָלַ֤ךְ
לְפָנֶ֙יךָ֙ צִדְקֶ֔ךָ כְּב֥וֹד יְהוָ֖ה
יַאַסְפֶֽךָ׃"
★ וּמְנוּחָתָם בְּגַן־עֵדֶן. אָמֵן.

Az yibbaḳaʿ kash-shaḥar orecha
vaʾaruchatecha mehera titsmaḥ, vehalach
lefanecha tsidḳecha, kevod Adonai
yaʾasfecha:
★ Umnuḥatam beGān ʿEden. Amen.

Then shall your light break forth like the morning, and your health shall spring forth speedily; and your righteousness shall go before you; the glory of Adonai will gather you in.
★ *May they rest in the Garden of Eden, Amen.*

A BLESSING BY PARENTS FOR THEIR SON

הָאֱלֹהִים אֲשֶׁר הִתְהַלְּכוּ אֲבוֹתֵינוּ,
אַבְרָהָם יִצְחָק, וְיַעֲקֹב, לְפָנָיו, הוּא
יְבָרֵךְ אוֹתְךָ לֵאמֹר: יְשִׂמְךָ אֱלֹהִים
כְּאֶפְרַיִם וְכִמְנַשֶּׁה: וְיִתֵּן
הָאֱלֹהִים לְךָ וּלְזַרְעֲךָ אִתָּךְ
אֶת־בִּרְכַּת אַבְרָהָם, וְיִשְׁמֹר אוֹתְךָ
וְיַצְלִיחַ דְּרָכֶיךָ וִימַלֵּא מִשְׁאֲלוֹת
לִבְּךָ לְטוֹבָה, וְיִתֵּן אֹשֶׁר וְאַהֲבָה
בֵּינֵינוּ בַּמִּשְׁפָּחָה. וִיהִי יְהוָֹה
אֱלֹהֵינוּ עִמְּךָ וְיִתֵּן לְךָ חָכְמָה
וּבִינָה וְיִהְיֶה לְבָבְךָ שָׁלֵם עִם
יְהוָֹה אֱלֹהֵינוּ, טָהוֹר וְזַךְ, לָלֶכֶת
בְּחֻקָּיו, לִשְׁמֹר מִצְווֹתָיו, לַעֲשׂוֹת
חֶסֶד, צְדָקָה וּמִשְׁפָּט:
★ אָמֵן.

Ha'Elohim asher hit-hallechu avotenu,
Avraham, Yitsḥaḳ, veYa'aḳov, lefanav, hu
yevarech otecha lemor: Yesimcha Elohim
ke'Efrayim vechiMnash-shé: Veyitten
Ha'Elohim lecha ulzar'acha ittecha
et birkat Avraham, veyishmor otecha
veyatsliaḥ derachecha vimallé mishalot
libbecha letova, veyitten osher ve'ahava
benenu bammishpaḥa. Vihi Adonai
Elohenu 'immecha veyitten lecha ḥochma
uvina veyihyé levavecha shalem 'im
Adonai Elohenu, tahor vezach, lalechet
beḥuḳḳav, lishmor mitsvotav, la'asot
ḥesed, tsedaḳa umishpat.
★ Amen.

MAY THE GOD, *before Whom my fathers Avraham, Yitshak, and Ya'akov walked, bless you and make you like Ephraim and like Menashe. And may God give you and your seed with you the blessings of Avraham, and save you, and make your ways successful, and make all your wishes come true for good, and grant joy and love among us in the family. And may Adonai be with you and give you wisdom and understanding, and may your heart be perfect with Adonai, our God, pure and clean, to walk in His statutes, and to keep His commandments to do kindness, charity, and justice.*
★ *Amen.*

A BLESSING BY PARENTS FOR THEIR SONS

הָאֱלֹהִים אֲשֶׁר הִתְהַלְּכוּ אֲבוֹתֵינוּ,
אַבְרָהָם, יִצְחָק וְיַעֲקֹב, לְפָנָיו, הוּא
יְבָרֵךְ אֶתְכֶם לֵאמֹר: יְשִׂימְכֶם
אֱלֹהִים כְּאֶפְרַיִם וְכִמְנַשֶּׁה:
וְיִתֵּן הָאֱלֹהִים לָכֶם וּלְזַרְעֲכֶם
אִתְּכֶם אֶת־בִּרְכַּת אַבְרָהָם, וְיִשְׁמֹר
אֶתְכֶם וְיַצְלִיחַ דַּרְכֵיכֶם וִימַלֵּא
מִשְׁאֲלוֹת לִבְּכֶם לְטוֹבָה וְיִתֵּן אֹשֶׁר
וְאַהֲבָה בֵּינֵינוּ בַּמִּשְׁפָּחָה. וִיהִי
יְהֹוָה אֱלֹהֵינוּ עִמָּכֶם וְיִתֵּן
לָכֶם חָכְמָה וּבִינָה וְיִהְיֶה לְבַבְכֶם
שָׁלֵם עִם יְהֹוָה אֱלֹהֵינוּ, טָהוֹר וְזַךְ,
לָלֶכֶת בְּחֻקָּיו, לִשְׁמֹר מִצְווֹתָיו,
לַעֲשׂוֹת חֶסֶד, צְדָקָה וּמִשְׁפָּט:
★ אָמֵן

Ha'Elohim asher hit-hallechu avotenu,
Avraham, Yitsḥaḳ, veYaʿaḳov, lefanav, hu
yevarech etchem lemor: Yesimechem
Elohim ke'Efrayim vechiMnash-shé:
Veyitten Ha'Elohim lachem ulzarʿachem
ittechem et birkat Avraham, veyishmor
etchem veyatsliaḥ darchechem vimallé
mishalot libbechem letova, veyitten osher
ve'ahava benenu bammishpaḥa. Vihi
Adonai Elohenu ʿimmachem veyitten
lachem ḥochma uvina veyihyé levavchem
shalem ʿim Adonai Elohenu, tahor vezach,
lalechet beḥuḳḳav, lishmor mitsvotav,
laʿasot ḥesed, tsedaḳa umishpat.
★ Amen.

MAY THE GOD, before Whom my fathers Avraham, Yitshak, and Ya'akov walked, bless you and make you like Ephraim and like Menashe. And may God give you and your seed with you the blessings of Avraham, and save you, and make your ways successful, and make all your wishes come true for good, and grant joy and love among us in the family. And may Adonai be with you and give you wisdom and understanding, and may your heart be perfect with Adonai, our God, pure and clean, to walk in His statutes, and to keep His commandments to do kindness, charity, and justice.

★ *Amen.*

A BLESSING BY PARENTS FOR THEIR DAUGHTER

הָאֱלֹהִים אֲשֶׁר הִתְהַלְּכוּ אֲבוֹתֵינוּ,	Ha'Elohim asher hit-hallechu avotenu,
אַבְרָהָם, יִצְחָק וְיַעֲקֹב, לְפָנָיו,	Avraham, Yitsḥaḳ, veYa'aḳov, lefanav,
הוּא יְבָרֵךְ אוֹתָךְ לֵאמֹר: יְשִׂימֵךְ	hu yevarech otach lemor: Yesimech
אֱלֹהִים כְּרוּת, אֵשֶׁת הַחַיִל, וּכְרָחֵל	Elohim keRut, eshet haḥayil, uchRaḥel
וּכְלֵאָה, אֲשֶׁר בָּנוּ שְׁתֵּיהֶם	uchLe'a, asher banu shtehem
אֶת־בֵּית יִשְׂרָאֵל: וְיִתֵּן הָאֱלֹהִים	et bet Yisra'el: Veyitten Ha'Elohim
לָךְ וּלְזַרְעֵךְ אִתָּךְ אֶת־בִּרְכַּת	lach ulzar'ech ittach et birkat
אַבְרָהָם, וְיִשְׁמֹר אוֹתָךְ וְיַצְלִיחַ	Avraham, veyishmor otach veyatsliaḥ
דְּרָכַיִךְ וִימַלֵּא מִשְׁאֲלוֹת לִבֵּךְ	derachayich vimallé mishalot libbech
לְטוֹבָה, וְיִתֵּן אֹשֶׁר וְאַהֲבָה בֵּינֵינוּ	letova, veyitten osher ve'ahava benenu
בַּמִּשְׁפָּחָה. וִיהִי יְהוָה אֱלֹהֵינוּ	bammishpaḥa. Vihi Adonai Elohenu
עִמָּךְ וְיִתֵּן לָךְ חָכְמָה וּבִינָה	'immach veyitten lach ḥochma uvina
וְיִהְיֶה לְבָבֵךְ שָׁלֵם עִם יְהוָה	veyihyé levavech shalem 'im Adonai
אֱלֹהֵינוּ, טָהוֹר וְזַךְ, לָלֶכֶת בְּחֻקָּיו,	Elohenu, tahor vezach, lalechet beḥuḳḳav,
לִשְׁמֹר מִצְוֹתָיו, לַעֲשׂוֹת חֶסֶד,	lishmor mitsvotav, la'asot ḥesed,
צְדָקָה וּמִשְׁפָּט:	tsedaḳa umishpat.
★ אָמֵן.	★ Amen.

MAY THE GOD, *before Whom my fathers Avraham, Yitshak, and Ya'akov walked, bless you and make you like Ruth, the woman of valor, and like Rachel and Leah, both of whom built the house of Israel. And may God give you and your seed with you the blessings of Avraham, and save you, and make your ways successful, and make all your wishes come true for good, and grant joy and love among us in the family. And may Adonai be with you and give you wisdom and understanding, and may your heart be perfect with Adonai, our God, pure and clean, to walk in His statutes, and to keep His commandments to do kindness, charity, and justice.*

★ *Amen.*

A BLESSING BY PARENTS FOR THEIR DAUGHTERS

הָאֱלֹהִים אֲשֶׁר הִתְהַלְּכוּ אֲבוֹתֵינוּ,	Ha'Elohim asher hit-hallechu avotenu,
אַבְרָהָם, יִצְחָק וְיַעֲקֹב, לְפָנָיו,	Avraham, Yitsḥaḳ, veYaʿaḳov, lefanav,
הוּא יְבָרֵךְ אֶתְכֶן לֵאמֹר: יְשִׂימְכֶן	hu yevarech etchen lemor: Yesimechen
אֱלֹהִים כְּרוּת, אֵשֶׁת הַחַיִל,	Elohim keRut, eshet haḥayil,
וּכְרָחֵל וּכְלֵאָה, אֲשֶׁר בָּנוּ שְׁתֵּיהֶם	uchRaḥel uchLe'a, asher banu shtehem
אֶת־בֵּית יִשְׂרָאֵל: וְיִתֵּן הָאֱלֹהִים	et bet Yisra'el: Veyitten Ha'Elohim
לָכֶן וּלְזַרְעֲכֶן אִתְּכֶן אֶת־בִּרְכַּת	lachen ulzarʿachen ittechen et birkat
אַבְרָהָם, וְיִשְׁמֹר אֶתְכֶן וְיַצְלִיחַ	Avraham, veyishmor etchen veyatsliaḥ
דַּרְכֵיכֶם וִימַלֵּא מִשְׁאֲלוֹת לִבְּכֶן	darchechen vimallé mish'alot libbechen
לְטוֹבָה וְיִתֵּן אֹשֶׁר וְאַהֲבָה בֵּינֵינוּ	letova, veyitten osher ve'ahava benenu
בַּמִּשְׁפָּחָה. וִיהִי יְהֹוָה אֱלֹהֵינוּ	bammishpaḥa. Vihi Adonai Elohenu
עִמָּכֶן וְיִתֵּן לָכֶן חָכְמָה וּבִינָה	ʿimmachen veyitten lachen ḥochma uvina
וְיִהְיֶה לְבַבְכֶן שָׁלֵם עִם יְהֹוָה	veyihyé levavechen shalem ʿim Adonai
אֱלֹהֵינוּ, טָהוֹר וְזַךְ, לָלֶכֶת בְּחֻקָּיו,	Elohenu, tahor vezach, lalechet beḥuḳḳav,
לִשְׁמֹר מִצְווֹתָיו, לַעֲשׂוֹת חֶסֶד,	lishmor mitsvotav, laʿasot ḥesed,
צְדָקָה וּמִשְׁפָּט:	tsedaḳa umishpat.
אָמֵן ★	★ Amen.

MAY THE GOD, *before Whom my fathers Avraham, Yitshak, and Ya'akov walked, bless you and make you like Ruth, the woman of valor, and like Rachel and Leah, both of whom built the house of Israel. And may God give you and your seed with you the blessings of Avraham, and save you, and make your ways successful, and make all your wishes come true for good, and grant joy and love among us in the family. And may Adonai be with you and give you wisdom and understanding, and may your heart be perfect with Adonai, our God, pure and clean, to walk in His statutes, and to keep His commandments to do kindness, charity, and justice.*

★ *Amen.*